PAKISTAN
Engagement of the Extremes

PAKISTAN
Engagement of the Extremes

Ashutosh Misra

Institute for Defence Studies and Analyses
New Delhi

SHIPRA

ISBN: 978-81-7541-431-0

First Published in India in 2008

Pakistan: Engagement of the Extremes

Published by :
SHIPRA PUBLICATIONS
115-A, Vikas Marg, Shakarpur, Delhi-110092 (India)
Tel. : 91-11-65277210, 22500954, Fax : 91-11-22458662
Email : info@shiprapublications.com
www.shiprapublications.com

Pakistan is like Israel. Take out Judaism from Israel and it will collapse like a house of cards. Take Islam out of Pakistan and make it a secular state, it would collapse.

–General Zia-ul Haq, President of Pakistan 1977-1988

Dedicated to
the fond memories of my late father
Ramesh Chandra Misra

Preface

Pakistan is a crucial country in the international system. Yet we do not know enough about it. Since the tragic events of September 11, 2001 and in the ensuing years, as matters in Iraq and more lately Afghanistan have turned more complex and violent, the place of Pakistan has only grown in importance. Pakistan in the past two years has been under tremendous internal stress and churning and at a very brisk pace, too. The spread in extremism from the tribal areas to other parts of Pakistan and General Pervez Musharraf's iron–fisted approach, including the crackdown on Lal Masjid, and the purging of the judiciary have only created more resistance to his rule. If the Lal Masjid operation infuriated the Islamist forces, the crackdown on the judiciary alienated civil-society and the common man. Musharraf's eventual resignation from the post of Chief of Army Staff and his controversial re-election as a civilian President, facilitated by a brief period of emergency rule, dented his popularity and legitimacy even further. His equivocations on holding elections and in allowing two former prime ministers to return to Pakistan caused the country to boil. Not surprisingly, the international community's worries about Pakistan have continued to grow.

With the return of Benazir Bhutto and Nawaz Sharif to Pakistan in November 2007, there was hope that a political opening might occur. Unfortunately, with the assassination of Benazir Bhutto, Pakistan appears to be headed towards more uncertainty and violence. The decision to go ahead with the general elections, with a slight delay, in February 2008, is a bold one. With Benazir Bhutto's death, the political arena has been drastically altered. Will the PPP come to power with the benefit of a sympathy wave in the aftermath of Benazir's death? Will Nawaz Sharif become the focal point of the struggle for democracy now and rise to power? Or will the ruling PML-Q retain its standing? What is the future of the Islamist parties? Will they lose or gain power?

Ashutosh Misra's book on the military and Islamic extremism in Pakistan is a timely endeavour. The manuscript was completed quite sometime ago and therefore recent events do not find a mention in it. Nonetheless, this is an extremely useful book as it provides the reader with valuable insights into the relationship between the military and the Islamists, which of course is an issue of great importance for the future, as well. Misra argues forcefully that the future of Pakistan will revolve around the two pivots of the military and the Islamists. The third pivot is that of the more liberal democratic elements in Pakistan comprising the major political parties and certain segments of civil society. A book that deals with the first two pivots must engage our attention. Misra has shown convincingly, and in detail, that they have been intertwined, that the military and the Islamists have been in conflict but have also cooperated.

How long and in what measure the two will continue to be in conflict and to cooperate in the future is of course the key question. Pakistan's own more indigenous Islamists are being influenced and "infiltrated" by the more Talibanized elements of Afghanistan and other foreign countries operating in and around Pakistan. They have shown, in their increasing boldness of action and speech that they are a huge force in Pakistan. Will they cause greater conflict with the military or will they live in some, howsoever uneasy, cohabitation with the military? To what extent will the Pakistani military, so closely wedded to the Islamists from the Zia period onwards, find itself in confrontation with the former allies and ideological partners, particularly with the United States and Western countries breathing down their necks?

The answer to these questions are in the future. To get an inkling into the future, one has to have a sense of the past. Misra's book traces through the linkages between the two major pivots in the past and points us towards an understanding if not prognosis of the future. The author has written on India-Pakistan relations, in particular, how the two countries have managed to fashion seasons of cooperation despite their conflicts. He has been a keen Pakistan watcher. Indians discuss Pakistan a great deal and have strong views on their troubled neighbour. Not many bother to write books on the subject. Misra has done so and has given us an interesting volume at a time when Pakistan is boiling.

Dehradun **Kanti P. Bajpai**
January 2008

Acknowledgements

This book is the culmination of my four and a half year of research association with the Institute for Defence Studies and Analyses (IDSA). I came to the Institute as a pure academician after my PhD from the Jawaharlal Nehru University (JNU), New Delhi and a stint at the United Nations University's Leadership Academy in Jordan and learnt the art of doing policy oriented research. I always consider IDSA to be the best place in the field in India for pursuing research in security and strategic studies. Despite being an autonomous institution IDSA's perceived image as a 'government' institution gives that extra push to its faculty to undertake serious policy oriented research work. I must say that IDSA certainly gave me the profile and exposure and brought me in contact with the policy makers, diplomats, bureaucrats, defence and para-military personnel, academicians and the leading analysts in the field in India and abroad which benefited me with the valuable narratives and also enriched my understanding of the subject a great deal.

I offer my gratitude towards the present Director Narendra Sisodia for his support and encouragement to stretch that extra bit which makes the difference in the end. He has been a great motivator behind my publishing this book. Besides, Virendra Gupta, Deputy Director, IDSA and South Asia Cluster Coordinator has been very supportive, as well. Under his guidance, perhaps I learnt the nuances of foreign policy imperatives and the tact to make the point without being too aggressive and blunt. My regular interactions with him and his insights in cluster meetings have been very rewarding on a range of issues pertaining to South Asia and larger foreign policy and security issues.

I thank K. Santhanam, former Director General, IDSA for having faith in my abilities and encouraging me to undertake research on even the most challenging of subjects. His hard-work and dedication to work itself has been a great motivator for young scholars like me. The former Deputy Director C. Uday Bhaskar also deserves a special note of acknowledgement for being an excellent South Asia Cluster Coordinator to which I belonged. From him I learnt the skill to do trapeze with facts while doing the analysis. Also, my research papers at IDSA would not have been rich in both content and analysis without the valuable inputs of my cluster colleagues, especially Ashok Behuria, for which I thank them in utmost earnest and sincerity.

During my IDSA years I must say that my works on Pakistan would not have taken the desired shape without the valuable inputs and comments of Kalim Bahadur, A.R. Deo, G. Parthasarthy, and Afsir Karim. They need a special mention since the final shape which this book has taken has been largely because of their important insights and remarks. A special vote of thanks also go to Kanti P. Bajpai, former Professor, Jawaharlal Nehru University for his insights on Pakistan.

At IDSA I am also very grateful to the editorial team comprising of Sujit Dutta, Uttam Sinha and Vivek Kaushik for doing an excellent job in editing my book and polishing it with finesse. The library staff of IDSA had a major role to play in helping me acquire the required research material on most occasions at instant notice and they deserve a special note of thanks, as well.

I also thank my publisher for making this book impeccable both, content and look-wise. Their copyediting has been thorough and rigorous which makes this book read elegantly.

I must also offer my appreciation for my two little sons, Srihan and Ruhan for having lived with my late homecomings and periodic outstation visits for conferences and seminars for over four years. At times, I accorded greater importance to my work at their expense which I hope they would understand as professional indispensability on part of their father, as they grow up. My mother has played a sheet anchor role in attending to their mischief and physically exhausting activities while my wife and I worked. She kept up with the demands of a modern lifestyle despite being a traditional woman. After my father's demise in 2001, while I was recuperating from the massive loss, my mother has been an amazing symbol of courage and inspiration which helped me overcome the tragedy and focus on my work.

My brother Paritosh and sister-in-law Patricia have been a constant source of support for me since my university days and have remained so which provided me with that vital sense of assurance should things go wrong. I have also learnt immensely from my father-in-law, Chintamani Pandey, former Inspector General of Police, Jammu and Kashmir. His insights on Jihad, Jihadis and their role in Pakistan and relationship with the Military have been something which I could not have gathered from any literature. By the same token, I must mention that Saurav Ray, Indian Defence Estate Officer and his experience as DEO J&K circle has contributed to my understanding of extremism and jihad, in Pakistan.

Last but not the least, my wife Sweta, I must say has been a formidable source of support and motivation and stood by me in my difficult days. Ever since our pre-mature return from Jordan in 2001 from my United Nations' assignment, due to family compulsions, her support has been like a rock of Gibraltar, helping me concentrate on my professional life. Many perhaps do not know that she has been the initial copy editor of my works before they were submitted or presented at IDSA and outside. I thank her for undertaking multipleroles as a wife, mother and senior editor with a publishing house simultaneously, and all with enormous good cheer.

I must say in the end that the views presented here are mine and no one but I am responsible for mistakes or errors, if any.

New Delhi
January 2008 **Ashutosh Misra**

Contents

Abbreviations

ANP	–	Awami National Party
ARD	–	Alliance for the Restoration of Democracy
AHP	–	Awami Himayat Tehrik
BoK	–	Bank of Pakistan
CDNS	–	Council for Defence and National Security
CENTO	–	Central Treaty Organization
CII-	–	Council for Islamic Ideology
C-in-C	–	Commander-in-Chief
CMLA	–	Chief Martial Law Administrator
COAS	–	Chief of Army Staff
CTFS	–	Commission on the Transformation of the Financial System
DHS	–	US Department of Homeland Security
FATA	–	Federally Administered Tribal Areas
FBI	–	Federal Bureau of Investigation
FSC	–	Federal Sharia Court
GHQ	–	General Headquarters
HuM	–	Harkat-ul-Mujahideen
ICAO	–	International Civil Aviation Organization
IJI	–	Islami Jamhoori Ittehad
IMF	–	International Monetary Fund
INS	–	US Immigration and Naturalisation Service
ISI	–	Inter-Services Intelligence
ITMD	–	Ittehad Tanzeematul Madaris al-Deeniya
J&K	–	Jammu and Kashmir

JAH	–	Jamiat Ahle Hadith
JCSC	–	Joint Chief of Staff Committee
JI	–	Jamaat-e-Islami
JKLF	–	Jammu Kashmir Liberation Front
JuD	–	Jamaat-ud-Dawa
JUH	–	Jamiat-e-Ulama-e-Hind
JUI	–	Jamiat-ul Islam
JUP	–	Jamiat-ul-Pakistan
JWP	–	Jamoohri Watan Party
LeJ	–	Lashkar-e-Jhangvi
LeT	–	Lashkar-e-Toiba
LFO	–	Legal Framework Order
MDM	–	Muttahida Deeni Mahaz
MMA	–	Muttahida Majlis-e-Amal
MQM	–	Mohajir Qaumi Movement
MQM	–	Muttahida Qaumi Movement
MRD	–	Movement for the Restoration for Democracy
PDA	–	Pakistan Democratic Alliance
PIF	–	Pakistan Islamic Front
IJM	–	Islami Jamhoori Mahaz
LeJ	–	Lashkar-e-Jhangvi
MYC	–	Milli Yakjehti Council
NADRA	–	National Database Registration Authority
NCPA	–	National Council of Pakistani Americans
NGO	–	Non-Governmental Organizations
NRB	–	National Reconstruction Bureau
NSC	–	National Security Council
NSC	–	Nifaz-e-Shariat Council
NSEERS	–	National Security Entry-Exit Registration System
PAT	–	Pakistan Awami Tehriq
PCO	–	Provisional Constitutional Order
PIT	–	Pakistan Islami Tehrik
PkMAP	–	Pushtoon-Khwa Milli Awami Party
PML-N	–	Pakistan Muslim League (Nawaz Sharif)
PML-Q	–	Pakistan Muslim League (Quaid-e-Azam)
PNA	–	Pakistan National Alliance

PoK	–	Pakistan Occupied Kashmir
PPP	–	Pakistan People's Party
PPP(S)	–	Pakistan People's Party (Aftab Sherapo)
PPPP	–	Pakistan People's Party Parliamentarian
RCO	–	Revival of Constitutional Order
SBP	–	State Bank of Pakistan
SEATO	–	South East Asian Treaty Organization
SSP	–	Sipah-e-Sahaba Pakistan
NWFP	–	North West Frontier Province
TeJ	–	Tehrik-e-Jafaria
TJ	–	Tablighi Jamaat
TNSM	–	Tanzeem-e-Nifaz-e-Shariat-e-Muhammadi
UJC	–	United Jihad Council
WB	–	World Bank

Introduction

Providing the Context

As a Pakistan watcher I have always believed that Pakistan's progress and growth since its birth, has largely been shaped by and under two kinds of extreme forces, though in varying degrees. The first extreme has seen the military having total control and influence over state affairs and the country's future, whereas the second extreme, though not as influential and powerful as the first, featured the Islamist parties and groups shaping Pakistan's Islamic character and inducing Islamic provisions in Constitution making. In some cases the Islamists charted an independent course such as the anti-Ahmediya movement and the protest to declare Pakistan as an Islamic state and forced the military regime to support their demands. In other cases, such as implementation of Sharia and other Islamic provisions, jihad in Afghanistan, and opposition to Western style democracy, they have chosen to rally behind various military regimes from time to time. Due to their weak electoral base the Islamist parties and groups have never enjoyed complete control over state affairs, until 2002 when they became a formidable political force with the military's support. Their potential to usurp state power under ripe conditions had never appeared as strong as in the post-2002 period and therefore need not be ignored casually. Their growing influence in moulding Pakistan's socio-political outlook and their sudden transformation from street power to political power qualifies them as the second extreme force. To their advantage, the moderate or the mainstream parties such as the Pakistan People's Party (PPP) and the Pakistan Muslim League-

Nawaz (PML-N), when in power, too have practiced a policy of appeasement to gain Islamic sanction for their rule and policies.

Under both the military and civilian regimes, the Islamists have had an important part to play in Pakistan's Constitution framing and identity creation processes. The reliance of the political elite on the Ulema, mosques and *madaris* (plural of *madrassa*) in interpreting Islamic terminology and its ideological metaphors emboldened their spirits and gave them a leeway to interfere in political processes. The Muslim League relied on Islam as a political tool during the freedom struggle to glue the Muslims together apropos Indian National Congress' vision of a 'secular' independent India. Ian Talbott has argued that Pakistan in the critical years following its creation was split between overlaps of regional, Pakistani and religious identities. Language and religion opened a pandora's box of these conflicting overlaps and failed to provide answers to the social, ethnic, religious and linguistic ills that marred Pakistan. Domination of Punjab, in decision-making and running affairs in addition to creation of highly centralized state structures, made people question the imposition of Pakistani nationalism. Increased authoritarianism in addition was of no help, or was rather indifferent to answering some very fundamental questions—which, whose and what Islam should be implemented and followed; the tendencies of the authoritarian elites to approach all dissent as a law and order problem rather than a political issue; manipulate and repress popular forces instead of accommodating their grievances; and accord preferential treatment to Punjab over other provinces diluted any chances of inclusive identity creation.[1] In the recent context, Prime Minister Shaukat Aziz's statement that **he is a Sunni** (emphasis added) Muslim showed the wide chasm that separates various sects and schools of Islamic jurisprudence in Pakistan. The enormity of General Musharraf's enlightened moderation can be assessed from the fact that even the Prime Minister has to categorically announce his religious leanings and faith.[2]

Much to Pakistan's dismay, the Muslim League, unlike the Indian National Congress, shared much of the criticism for not imparting any meaningful role in state and identity-building after 1947. It was rendered disoriented and rudderless to a great extent after the death of Quaid-e-Azam Muhammad Ali Jinnah and the assassination of Liaquat Ali Khan. The notion of Pakistan was conceived at the moment of the birth and lacked continuity.[3] It hampered the growth of a strong notion of nationalism in Pakistan. The elitist nature of the leadership and the multi-ethnic nature of Pakistan's social construct posed obstruction before identity creation in the years to come. The passing away of visionary leaders such as Muhammad Ali Jinnah and Liaquat Ali Khan, shortly after independence, hampered Constitution framing too, which proved detrimental to the establishment of democracy in the years to come. The Government of India Act of 1935 worked as a provisional Constitution of Pakistan until 1956 when the Constitution containing 234 Articles was passed by the second Constituent Assembly under the reign of Governor General Iskander Mirza and Prime Minister Chaudhary Muhammad Ali.[4] The 1956 Constitution endorsed and accommodated the views of the Ulema and declared Pakistan an Islamic Republic thus allowing the Ulema to have a say in state affairs. Yet, there remained considerable confusion over a definitive role for Islam in politics owing to the debate over 'whose Islam'?[5] According to Vali Nasr, "...state-led Islamization has allowed the state to organize, bolster the power of, and ultimately control institutions and social organizations that can allow it to use Islam in the services of state interests. Islamization allowed the state to reap the fruits of the Islamist propaganda and win the competition with the Islamist challenge from below to control the normative order, and thus construct a viable state ideology that provides for uniformity across society, as well as greater compliance with the will of the state".[6]

Pakistan has experienced over 30 years of existence under the extreme dominated by military dictatorships, elevating the military as a supra-national institution in social, political, economic and of course, the military sense. In a perfect combination of power domination and political machination, the Pakistani military since Field Marshal Ayub Khan's days till the present has enjoyed direct rule and while out of power, indirectly propped up and toppled democratic regimes arbitrarily with impunity. The military has crafted, tampered, suspended and kept the Constitution in abeyance on different occasions to suit its self-interests and projected itself as the sole guarantor of Pakistan's security, stability and progress. In its pursuit for power, the military had no qualms about exploiting the moderate parties, aligning with the Islamist parties and positioning them as a counter-balance to each other, when the situation demanded. Such a machination was largely facilitated by the failings and political rivalry of the moderate parties, mainly the PPP and the PML-N on the one hand, and limited political influence of the Islamist parties on the other. The Movement for the Restoration for Democracy (MRD), which later became the Alliance for the Restoration for the Democracy (ARD) were temporary phenomena and disintegrated soon after achieving their desired goals. They failed in evolving a democratic culture in Pakistan which could mobilize impromptu resistance at the national level against the military coups and onslaught on democratic regimes. Put wisely, the lack of a common understanding among the political parties, such as committing in principle to collectively oppose any unconstitutional dissolution of the National Assembly and declining any political arrangement or deal with the military at the cost of democracy, worked to the military's advantage. This lack of a substantial political protest in the wake of the imposition of martial law in 1958, 1969, 1977 and 1999 and repeated toppling of democratic regimes in the 1990s, is a grim reminder of the vulnerability of Pakistan's political parties and leaders to political opportunism. Zulfiqar Ali Bhutto did not protest against General Yahya Khan, the 1969 coup and being his trusted aide, to him the ends justified the means. Couple of decades later, when Nawaz Sharif' did not raise any voice of protest against Benazir Bhutto's sacking in 1990 and 1996, the latter returned the favour when Nawaz Sharif was sacked in 1993 and 1999. The failure of the PPP and PML-N regimes to deliver the goods and provide Pakistan with effective and clean governance subjected them to severe public criticism. It gave the President, who mostly acted at the behest of the military, the opportunity to press a long list of charges to justify the overthrow of the government. Between 1990 and 1999, the President charged the democratic regimes with undermining Pakistan's national interest and dissolved them with impunity on most occasions on template charges of corruption, nepotism, misgovernance, economic bankruptcy and disintegration. An analysis of the national address following the military coups by the military dictators, in chapter one, would reveal how the above template charges have been invoked to justify the military takeover, time and again.

Field Marshal Ayub Khan's despise for political leaders and the marginalization of democratic forces during his rule allowed the religious forces to fill in the ensuing political cavity. Despite being acknowledged as a secular person in his political and social conduct, his decision of invoking Islamic zeal among the soldiers and people, in the war against India in 1965, established Islam's indispensability in Pakistan's security considerations. It wrote a promising future for the Ulema and their pursuits for political power and influence in the years to come. After Ayub Khan's departure, the first formal understanding between the military and the Islamists was reached under General Yahya Khan in 1970 who co-opted them to counter the nationalists' agitation against military rule in both West and East Pakistan. Even after the end of the military rule in 1971 and the arrival of PPP supremo Zulfiqar Ali Bhutto, the exploitation of the Islam card by the political elite did not cease. Vali Nasr in his seminal work, *Islamic Leviathan* presents a comparative analysis of Islamization in Pakistan and Malaysia. In both the cases he has asserted that the state leaders (in this case Zulfiqar Ali Bhutto) believed that to claim support from Islamism and to exploit it for expanding state power, it was important that the state was construed as Islamic. Islamism or the ideology of Islam was useful in mobilizing new symbols, formulating new Islamic concepts of political relevance, which apart from serving political ends also appealed to the masses.[7] Husain Haqqani has argued that Islam has been the central theme in Pakistan's politics because of a conscious and consistent policy which went beyond its use in Afghanistan against the Soviet intervention, and aimed at marginalizing secular politicians from politics and maintaining a centralized control by the civil-military bureaucracy. Pakistan's self characterization as an Islamic and ideological state would remain unchanged for long and Islam would be used to bridge the differences between various ethnic and linguistic communities.[8]

Between 1971 and 1973, under the presidency of Zulfiqar Ali Bhutto, the 1973 Constitution was framed, which extensively enshrined the Islamic provisions. To appease the Islamists, Article 2 declared that Islam would be the state religion and Article 227 provided that all existing laws were to be framed in conformity with the injunctions of Islam.[9] Islamic teachings were made mandatory for Muslims and the Council of Islamic Ideology (CII) was created to suggest recommendations on Islamic matters to the government. By 1974 the sectarian strife had intensified and Bhutto was forced by the Ulema to declare Ahmediyas as non-Muslims.[10] This emboldened the Islamists and fed their appetite for more power influence in Pakistan. Although Islam has been a factor in Pakistan's political development, a source of national identity, legitimacy and social protest, many analysts believe that the definition and implementation of Muslim identity in Pakistani state and society has remained unambiguous. The Ahmediya affair and the 1956 Constitution revealed the interplay of Islamic identity and politics and that religion was more a source of conflict, and compromise than national unity.[11] The 1956 Constitution, declaring Pakistan as an Islamic state, asserted the relationship of Islam with reference to democracy rather delineating. In other words, the use of terms such as democracy, popular sovereignty, parliamentary political parties was only rhetorical in nature. By the same token many believed that the constant struggle to balance between an Islamic identity and democratic outlook for Pakistan produced the phenomena of 'rhetorical Islamization' which helps to explain why Pakistan's search of an Islamic identity has remained unsuccessful.[12] Yet, notwithstanding the ambiguity over the use of Islam and its role in Pakistan's history, regimes and leaders ceaselessly exploited it for image building and silencing their critics.

This was more visible under General Zia-ul-Haq who nurtured a highly Islamized and theocratic regime; both in terms of ideology and application. He stoked Islamic sentiments among the masses to counter the PPP propaganda to legitimize his martial law.[13] General Zia joined hands with the Jamaat-e-Islami (JI) to implement his Islamic agenda and vision for Pakistan. In addition to JI, several other orthodox Islamic leaders and their cadres started supporting

General Zia's Islamization policies. The controversial *Hudood* laws were passed in 1979 by a Presidential decree to bring certain aspects of the justice system pertaining to women (with regard to rape, consensual sexual intercourse, adultery and false accusation of these acts) in conformity with Islam. Between 1979-1985, because of their opposition to the democratic principles, particularly to the legislature elected on the basis of direct adult franchise, the Islamist parties and groups made a common cause with General Zia to mutual advantage. In the meantime, the Soviet Union had invaded Afghanistan and Pakistan was dragged into the cold war rivalry in its backyard. Jihad became the catch phrase and General Zia's military regime became increasingly preoccupied with Afghanistan. A force of jihadis to fight against the Soviets had become a necessity for both Pakistan and the United States. With American money, Pakistan under General Zia unleashed Jihad in Afghanistan and hoped that it would establish itself as the voice of the *umma* (Islamic community) and leader of the Islamic world. General Zia also intended to use Islam and jihad to silence the critics of his regime at home and convince the masses of his Islamic vision for Pakistan. As per the official figures, between 1979-82, 151 new *madaris* were created followed by another 1,000 between 1982-86.[14] According to Jamal Malik, "Increase in state patronage of religious seminaries in Pakistan in the 1980s showed that it was not so much an effort to placate Islamist activists or to give the state greater control through clientalism, as to use them as an outlet for conveying state ideology to the masses".[15] Democracy became the obvious casualty and protesting voices were lost, ignored and subdued underneath the cries of Jihad in Afghanistan. General Zia had become the frontline ally of the Americans against the Soviets and ushered 'Pakistan's drift into extremism', to borrow Hassan Abbas' phraseology.[16] General Zia's decision to follow the Islamization path was a conscious decision and a reaction to the growing political instability and ethnicity in politics in Balochistan, North West Frontier Province (NWFP), Sindh, and Southern Punjab. The ethno-national challenges were regarded by General Zia as going against the interest of the State. As per Vali Nasr's interpretation of Islamization, General Zia's policies were aimed at expanding State's hegemony and outreach, gaining more control over institutions including Islamic, mobilizing more people to support the State's political ideology and gain legitimacy as a truly Islamic State.

The convergence of interests between the military and the Islamists and their parallel power growth helps explain why after General Zia's death in 1988 and return of democracy, the Islamists became politically marginalized in the absence of State support. Their poor performance in the 1988, 1990, 1993, and 1996 elections in the National and Provincial Assemblies could have been far better had those elections been held under complete military control. However, their electoral defeat did not necessarily mean the end of the politics of Islam because both military and the moderate parties had busted the monopoly of the Islamists as the sole representatives of Islam and Islamization. This is perhaps one of the classic contradictions of Pakistan's democracy wherein even the moderate parties invoked Islamic principles in their pursuits of power and to such an extent that it blinded them to the adverse influence on democracy itself. In a political system where religion served such multiple purposes as mentioned in the preceding sections, and policies, laws, beliefs, political and social conducts were judged through the prism of religion, it became increasingly difficult beyond a point to reconcile it with democratic principles. This is not to question the sanctity of Islam in Pakistani life and politics, but merely to highlight the contradictions that have bedeviled democracy in Pakistan for decades.

As another phase of military-Ulema understanding began to unfold in the post-1999 period under General Musharraf, the 2002 general elections would become a watershed in Pakistan's political history. Their relationship achieved new heights accruing benefits to both on a reciprocal basis. Both depended heavily on each other and had a common adversary—the moderate parties and their struggle for the restoration of democracy. Under General Musharraf, the first of the military-Ulema joint ventures took shape in April 2002 before his Presidential Referendum. He ordered the release of a number of sectarian bigwigs, most notably among them, Maulana Azam Tariq, head of Sipah-e-Sahaba Pakistan (SSP), for political canvassing for his Referendum. This understanding carried right up to the October 2002 elections and thereafter it consolidated further. The rise of the religious parties in the October 2002 elections went a long way in facilitating General Musharraf's consolidation of power. Their support hinged on the unwritten understanding that General Musharraf would in turn ignore MMA's Islamic agenda and Islamization drive in the NWFP and Balochistan. Since 2002 Islamization has been pursued with vigour and purpose in the NWFP. The passing of the *Hisbah* and *Sharia* bills in the NWFP Assembly woke General Musharraf to the perils of Islamization taking the form of Talibanization with far-reaching consequences for Pakistan. To ward off any political instability in the National Assembly General Musharraf tended to ignore MMA's Islamization policies and his failure on the issue of madrassa registration and containing the Taliban dominance in the Federally Administered Tribal Area (FATA) show his regime's limitations in putting the genie back in the bottle. The linkage between the Jihadi groups, the military and the Inter-Services Intelligence (ISI) and evidences of their role in the unsuccessful assassination bids on General Musharraf's life indicated that decades of military-Islamist relationship had become hard to dismantle. Although General Musharraf did manage to halt the Islamization drive in the NWFP, it is believed to be a case of too little and too late. Islamists now lurk over General Musharraf's regime as a serious threat. Analysts argue that Pakistan does appear vulnerable to extreme Islamic eruptions with a backing from the military, on which this book builds a possibility of Islamists achieving far greater control than ever on shaping Pakistan's Islamic character.

General Musharraf was soon found grappling with ways to minimize the damage caused by his alignment with the Islamists. His policy of enlightened moderation is an effort at making Pakistan break out of the power structures of the Past based on military-Islamist partnership. In the process the resistance that he confronts reinforces the argument of Vali Nasr that "Islamism is not opposed to the state *per se* and its hegemony and control over economy and society, but to the secular ideology of the state"[17] which in this context is General Musharraf's enlightened moderation. General Musharraf's regime has been characterized by two distinct facets of state-led Islamization, within a short period. The first showed *convergence of interests* between the military and the Islamists evolving in early 2002, in a run-up to the April Presidential Referendum. There remained unanimity between both extremes over expanding State's hegemony and reach invoking Islamic principles in political practice. It was convenient for both the extremes to resist 'Western-style democracy' as championed by the moderate parties. The military condoned the establishment of democracy because it meant its retreat into the barracks and the Islamists disliked it because they feared dilution of their interpretation of *Sharia* laws, human rights, rights of women and minorities, education and other social practices. The second facet characterized *growing confrontation* between the military and the Islamists, primarily due to General Musharraf's alliance with West in the global war against terrorism and drive for enlightened moderation, both seen as anti-Islamic, if not secular, by the Islamist parties and the Jihadi groups.

This book is a product of my four years of research at the Institute for Defence Studies and Analyses (IDSA) in New Delhi where as a part of my parent project on civil-military relationship in Pakistan, I looked into the military-Islamist relationship and its impact on democracy. The following chapters revolve around the fundamental argument that General Musharraf's alliance with Islamists was not so much a reactionary approach, as much as it was a pro-active one, aimed at gaining legitimacy from the masses as an Islamic State and consolidating his military regime by using them in making inroads into the political strongholds of the moderate parties. The fundamental difference which this book discerns in the course of analysis between General Musharraf and General Zia-ul Haq is that, unlike the latter's full throttle Islamization policies seeing no limits in terms of formulation and implementation and association with the Islamists and jehadi groups, General Musharraf has chosen to reconsider his alliance with the Islamist lobby before Islamization transforms into Talibanization. It traces the relationship between the two extremes (military and the Islamists) and examines various measures and acts that resulted from their engagement since 2002. The book deals with the triad of military, Islamization and democracy and how these impact on Pakistan's long-term interests.

NOTES

1. Ian Talbott, *Pakistan A Modern History,* Oxford University Press, New Delhi, 1998, p. 1.
2. "I am a Sunni Muslim, says Shaukat", at http://www.dawn.com/2004/07/01/nat2.htm
3. Vali Nasr, *Islamic Leviathan: Islam and the Making of State Power,* Oxford University Press, New York, 2001, p. 25.
4. Ayesha Jalal, *The State of Martial Rule*, Cambridge University Press, Cambridge, 1990, p. 214.
5. Veena Kukreja, *Contemporary Pakistan: Political Processes, Conflicts and Crises*, Sage Publications, New Delhi, 2003, p. 163.
6. Vali Nasr, No. 3, p. 15.
7. *Ibid.*, p. 14.
8. Husain Haqqani, *Pakistan: Between Mosque and Military*, Vanguard Books, Lahore, 2005, p. 321.
9. Hassan Abbas, *Poleaxe or Politics of the Eighth Amendment 1985-1997,* Watandost, Lahore, 1997, p. 34.
10. *Ibid.*, p. 164.
11. John L. Esposito and John O. Voll, *Islam and Democracy,* Oxford University Press, Oxford, 1996, pp. 102-103.
12. Hamza Alvi, "Ethnicity, Muslim Society, and the Pakistan Ideology", in Anita M. Weiss, ed., *Islamic Reassertion in Pakistan*, Syracuse University Press, Syracuse, 1986, p. 44, Esposito and Voll, 1996, p. 105.
13. Begum Nusrat Bhutto vs. the Chief of Army Staff, etc. PLD, 1977, Supreme Court, pp. 657-763, in Hasan Askari Rizvi, *The Military and Politics in Pakistan*, Konark Publishers, New Delhi, 1988, p. 233.
14. "Pakistan: Madrasas, Extremism and the Military", International Crisis Group (ICG) Asia Report. No. 36. July 29, 2002, p. 9.
15. Jamal Malik, "Islamization in Pakistan in 1977-1985: The Ulama and Their Places of Learning," *Islamic Studies*, Vol. 28, No.1, Spring 1989, p. 23, cited in Vali Nasr, no. 3, p. 16.
16. Hassan Abbas, *Pakistan's Drift into Extremism: Allah, the Army and America's War on Terror*, M.E. Sharpe, New York, 2005.
17. Vali Nasr, no. 3, p. 14.

CHAPTER I

The First Extreme

Military's Rise and Rule in Pakistan

This chapter dwells upon the factors and conditions that facilitated the rise and unrelenting domination of the Military and how it created chances and prepared the ground for stepping into the political arena. It would go to examine how the civilian forces became subservient to the Military thereby creating a milieu in which the Military would confront little difficulty in functioning as the final arbiter of Constitution framing, decision and policy making and governance. Besides, the Military's own reputation as one of the biggest corporate houses in Pakistan is also a part of discussion in this chapter.

In the formative years of Pakistan following its creation, Muhammad Ali Jinnah and Liaquat Ali Khan donned the mantle of State, identity and institution-building. For this they deemed the control over the bureaucracy essential, which was largely the case initially under Muhammad Ali Jinnah and then under Liaquat Ali Khan until his death in 1951. After the death of Muhammad Ali Jinnah and the assassination of Liaquat Ali Khan there remained no visionary of their stature who could have wrested control of their unfinished tasks and thereafter the civil-military oligarchy became central to the State and institution-building tasks. Between 1947 and 1958 the power coterie—which consisted of senior civil servants and civil servant-turned politicians—maintained close links with the Military primarily for dealing with security and law and order matters. There was no Constitution which could have laid down rules, laws and procedures for rights, codes of conduct and duties for different office-bearers. The Government of India Act of 1935 with some modifications and amendments acted as the provisional Constitution. As a result, following Liaquat Ali Khan's assassination in October 1951, and the ambiguity over the rights and duties of the Governor-General and the Prime Minister, there ensued a tussle between Governor General Ghulam Mohammad and Prime Minister Nazimuddin. When Nazimuddin attempted to harness the powers of Ghulam Mohammad, the latter unceremoniously sacked him in April 1953, dismissed the Constituent Assembly and formed his own 'cabinet of talents'. The new cabinet was a mere eyewash and nothing short of a 'constitutional dictatorship'.[1] It heralded a new chapter in Pakistan's history in which the civil-military oligarchy would join hands to run Pakistan and keep their own interests supreme.

Military's Entry into Politics

In this new political dispensation, Ghulam Muhammad became Governor-General and Mohammad Ali Bogra, a minor political figure from East Bengal by virtue of being the Prime Minister who had also approved of the dissolution of the Constituent Assembly, headed the 'Cabinet of talents'. Chaudhary Mohammad Ali, former head of the Civil Services of Pakistan, became the Finance Minister, but above all, General Mohammad Ayub Khan, Commander-in-Chief of the Army, was inducted as the Defence Minister. It was the first instance of the Army Chief occupying twin positions and Ghulam Mohammad paved the way for the Military to get directly involved in politics and went on to marginalize the role of Prime Minister in decision making. So while the civil-Military oligarchy governed Pakistan, eight precious years passed without much progress on Constitution framing, more so due to discord over political and financial rights of the centre and provinces. Eventually, when a Federal Constitution actually came into force on March 23, 1956, the Military by then had made enough incursions into the political system to subvert the evolving constitutional set up. Although the first Constitution of 1956 envisaged a parliamentary form of government, it concentrated powers in the hand of the President empowering him to dissolve the National Assembly (NA) and appoint the Prime Minister.[2] Also, the

Constituent Assembly which was entrusted with the task of framing the Constitution had feudal lords in majority to its disadvantage who successfully thwarted adoption of land reforms, which till date impinges on the democratic setup in Pakistan. The ensuing political bickering and confusion made it difficult for the political forces to run the State affairs smoothly and in 1958 Field Marshal Ayub Khan imposed Martial Law. Later, he abrogated the Constitution and tailored another Constitution in 1962, specifically designed to legitimize and consolidate Military's hold over political power. His dislike for political parties and their leaders could not be kept under wraps for long. After the coup in 1958, Ayub depicted the "political leaders as bringing the country to its knees through their misuse of power, corruption and factional intrigue" which in one stroke sought to establish the incapability of the civilian forces and indispensability of the Military to assume charge.[3]

In 1959, Ayub Khan banned political parties and purged the 'troublemakers' through the Public (Disqualification) Order (PODO) and the Elective Bodies (Disqualification) Order (EBDO). These measures gave the former politicians the option of trial or voluntary withdrawal from public service. He introduced 'basic democracy' through the Basic Democracy Order, a five-tier system or representation from Rural Union Councils and Urban Union Committees, through the *Thana* or *Tehsil* Committee, to the District and Divisional Councils and ultimately to two Provincial Development Advisory Councils. In total 80,000 Basic Democrats were slotted to reach the union council and committees in the new party-less democratic system, wherein a Basic Democrat represented a population of 10,000 to 15,000.[4] These democrats elected Ayub Khan twice as President in 1960 and 1965. It would be fair to say that Ayub Khan was seen as a reformist and hardheaded administrator for his measures which also included crackdown on the hoarders, black-marketers and smugglers. In the end, Ayub Khan's idea of 'basic democracy' as a substitute for parliamentary democracy, failed due to over-reliance on the bureaucracy for its execution.[5]

Under Ayub Khan the secessionist movement in East Pakistan was getting stronger and eventually he had to request the Military under General Yahya Khan to step in and gain control of the situation. General Yahya Khan imposed Martial Law on March 25, 1969 and promulgated the Legal Framework Order (LFO) on March 30 setting a deadline of 120 days to frame another Constitution. All this had little effect on the nationalist unrest in East Pakistan. Yahya Khan announced elections to be held in October 1970 which were eventually held in December due to natural calamities that had hit East Pakistan. The Awami League of Sheikh Mujibur Rehman swept the elections, winning 80 seats followed by Qayyum Muslim League (70 seats), Muslim League (Daultana, 40 seats), National Awami Party (Wali, 35 seats) and PPP (25 seats).[6] The results came as a blow for the West Pakistan leadership and an adamant Yahya Khan refused to convene the National Assembly session for it meant that not only a larger (in terms of elected members) East Pakistan-based political party would dominate the National Assembly over the West Pakistan-based PPP but have its own Prime Minister as well. Several rounds of negotiations between Yahya Khan and Mujibur Rehman on the one hand, and Z. A Bhutto and Mujibur Rehman on the other, failed to yield any compromise between East and West Pakistan. Mujibur Rehman simply refused to budge on the six-point demands which included federal and parliamentary form of government, autonomy of affairs except defence and foreign policy, separate mutually convertible currencies, autonomy of fiscal polices, separate accounts for foreign exchange earnings and right to raise a militia or a para-military force.[7] Now Mujibur Rehman put a price on his party attending the National Assembly session. In March 1971, Mujibur Rehman as a pre-condition he put forward another set of demands including immediate withdrawal of Martial Law; transfer of power to the elected representatives of the people; immediate withdrawal of all military personnel to the barracks; immediate cessation of the transfer of troops from West Pakistan to East Bengal; immediate cessation of firing on civilians; non-interference by the military authorities in Bangladesh; and maintenance of law and order to be undertaken by Bengali East Pakistan Rifles and sometimes Awami League volunteers.[8] Riots broke out between Urdu and Bengali-speaking communities and East Pakistan was engulfed in fierce clashes.

Subsequently, it took shape of a civil war when General Yahya Khan ordered the West Pakistan-led Army to launch 'Operation Searchlight' to quell the rebellion. Mujibur Rehman was arrested while he was in West Pakistan in connection with negotiations. Eventually, with the help of *Mukti Bahini* (Liberation Force) from India, the West Pakistan Military surrendered on December 16, 1971 and East Pakistan became independent as Bangladesh. In West Pakistan, the Supreme Court declared Yahya Khan's Martial Law illegal and Zulfiqar Ali Bhutto became the President on December 20, 1971, ending General Yahya Khan's and the military's shortest rule in Pakistan.

Under Zulfiqar Ali Bhutto Pakistan got a new Constitution on August 14, 1973 and party-based general elections were held, making him the first popularly elected Prime Minister. The new Constitution concentrated powers in the hands of the Prime Minister. It introduced a bicameral system; proclaimed Islam as a state religion (Article 227); made the President act as per the 'binding' advice of the Prime Minister (Article 48), among other provisions, which strengthened the system of parliamentary democracy. The most significant aspect of the Constitution was the role defined for the Military in state affairs. Article 245 (1) explicitly mentioned, "Armed forces shall, under the direction of the Federal Government, defend Pakistan against external aggression or threat of war, and subject to Law, act in aid of civil power when called upon to do so."[9] Article 6 further specified, "Any person who abrogates or attempts or conspires to abrogate, subverts or attempts or conspires to subvert the Constitution by use of force or show of force or by other unconstitutional means shall be guilty of high treason."[10] In September 1973, Parliament approved another law [Article 6(3)], which prescribed the death penalty for committing the acts prohibited through Article 6.[11]

In due course Zulfiqar Ali Bhutto became unpopular for his political brinkmanship and authoritarian style of leadership. Apart from the agitation by the traders and merchants against the nationalization of industries, the anti-Bhutto wave was being fuelled by the resentment of the urban middle class against the deterioration in educational standards. In the wake of the announcement for national and provincial elections in 1977, the nine-party Pakistan

National Alliance (PNA) was founded to take on Bhutto's campaign over inflation, government arbitrariness and unemployment and the creation of *Nizam-e-Mustafa*. Like the 1969 anti-Ayub agitation, this time too, small businessmen and students were at the forefront.[12] In the subsequent elections allegations of widespread rigging to ensure PPP's victory made Bhutto more unpopular. Sensing an opportunity, General Zia-ul-Haq drew curtains on the government on July 5, 1977. To escape the charges of 'high treason' Zia-ul-Haq did not abrogate the 1973 Constitution, but only kept it in abeyance. Aware of the political base and following of Bhutto, Zia was in no mood to spare his life. A subdued and fearful judiciary, acting on Zia's directives, ruled the hanging of Bhutto on April 4, 1979.

As the Chief Martial Law Administrator, General Zia in his July 5, 1977 National Address tried to dispel public fear and promised to hold 'free and fair' elections in the following October, but later deferred the promise. Much to General Zia's good fortunes, Soviet Union invaded Afghanistan in 1979, which diverted the attention of the public from internal political wrangling to outside Pakistan. To tighten his stranglehold over power, General Zia transferred the Chief Justice of the Supreme Court to deter the judiciary and to rule out the possibility of the apex court setting a deadline for elections. To consolidate himself legally, General Zia promulgated the Provisional Constitutional Order (PCO) on March 24, 1981, which rendered the courts completely marginalized and ineffective. The Press was banned and all papers were shut down through the 'Press advice' and Press-censorship' measures. In 1984 General Zia held a Referendum as a stamp of approval for his autocratic rule. Official reports showed 60 per cent voters rushing to the booth to give the seal of approval. The true story of the Referendum was published by *The Muslim* and was therefore immediately ordered to be withdrawn from the market.[13]

Devoid of the participation of the major political parties, general elections were finally held in February 1985, followed by the Revival of Constitutional Order (RCO) issued on March 2, 1985, which sought to alter the basic tenets of the 1973 Constitution. As many as sixty-five Articles were either amended or substituted and the puppet

Prime Minister Mohammad Khan Junejo was forced to accept it as a trade-off for lifting of Martial Law. Thus, was the draconian Eighth Amendment inserted into the Constitution. The Bill was laid for approval and passed by the Senate in just four days on November 14, 1985 and the National Assembly took 19 days to pass it. Article 58 (2)(b) of the Eighth Amendment gave the President the powers to dissolve the National Assembly when in his opinion the government was not able to function constitutionally.[14] The President secured the right to nominate the Prime Minister, governors of the provinces, and judges of High Courts and the Supreme Court, including the Chief Justice, and the Prime Minister became subservient to the President. Article 58 (2)(b) was invoked by Zia-ul-Haq in 1988, Ghulam Ishaq Khan in 1990 and 1993, and Farooq Leghari in 1996.

Military's Tactical Retreat (1988-93)

General Zia-ul Haq's rift with the government became evident when he sacked Junejo's government in 1988. Unexpectedly, General Zia died in a plane crash in 1988 which gave Benazir Bhutto and the movement for democracy a huge fillip. She was mobilizing the Pakistan People's Party in a big way and in the general elections on November 17, 1988 with the support of Muttahida Qaumi Movement (MQM) she formed the government. However, within two years, her differences with President Ghulam Ishaq Khan on the issues of retirement of Admiral Sirohey, the Joint Chief of Staff Committee; appointment of judges; and the appointment of governor for NWFP became Pronounced. As a result Ghulam Ishaq Khan on the grounds of corruption, nepotism, internal dissension in the political parties leading to malfunctioning of the National Assembly, and disregarding the interests of the provincial assemblies, dismissed her government on August 6, 1990, declaring a state of Emergency.

Ghulam Mustafa Jatoi became the caretaker Prime Minister and elections were held on October 24 and 27, 1990, which saw the Islamic Jamhoori Ittehad (IJI) defeat the PPP that brought Nawaz Sharif to power as Prime Minister. As a change in regime could never have been a panacea for the political woes of the country, differences emerged between the President and Nawaz Sharif on the appointment of the new Army Chief to replace General Aslam Beg; privatization of Muslim commercial banks; and the Eighth Amendment.[15] Hectic parleys between IJI and PPP and Nawaz's patch up efforts with the President failed to save the government. He was sacked on April 18, 1993.

Failings of the 'Democrats': Military's Favourite Theme (1993-99)

Yet another general election was foisted on the nation in October 1993, which brought Benazir Bhutto back to power. On November 13, 1993, PPP supported Farooq Leghari for the Presidency to secure itself against future presidential adventurism. The move did not benefit Benazir. After merely two years of co-existence Benazir Bhutto and Farooq Leghari became rivals and the latter sacked her government on November 5, 1996. Again, among other issues, the appointment of the new Army Chief was the bone of contention, which speaks eloquently about the salience of the position of Chief of Army Staff (COAS) in politics. The government was dismissed on standard 'template' charges of corruption, malfunctioning and nepotism, and conspiracy to kill Murtaza Bhutto, and the government's interference with the appointments of the civil servants and judges. Ayesha Jalal, while acknowledging the politician's chaotic behaviour, indiscipline and corruption for hampering effective governance, blames the bureaucrats and the generals more for Pakistan's woes and erosion of democracy through their intervention.[16] In contrast, Hassan Abbas absolves the bureaucracy and Military of the charges of grabbing power and blames the political elite for making the political forces subservient to the Military and bureaucracy. He writes,

> *The argument that bureaucracy and Military grabbed power from politicians is absurd. Government reliance on bureaucracy for the rehabilitation of migrants from India, and dependence on Military due to Indian threat were not reasons enough for political forces to become subservient to civil-Military bureaucracy. Had there been a 'congenial constitution' in force, the political elements would have reigned supreme. The Commander-in-Chief of Pakistan Army was*

> *inducted in the Cabinet in 1954 to gain Army's support for the ruling elite. The politicians who committed this unforgivable sin set the trend for which the nation is paying through its nose to this day. It provided Army with a chance to have direct say in governmental affairs. Army never surrendered the privilege.*[17]

On February 7, 1997 Nawaz Sharif returned to power with a thumping majority. In his second term, Nawaz Sharif's, priorities were—abolishing the Eighth Amendment and insulating his government against the Council for Defence and National Security (CDNS), which was set up by Farooq Leghari through the Presidential Decree of January 1997. The CDNS was created with the purpose of advising the government on vital matters and enhancing the Military's role in politics. Much to the credit of Nawaz Sharif and his strong position in the Parliament, on "Fool's day", April 1, 1997 one of the most historic and wisest acts of Pakistan's political history was given shape by a civilian government—the Thirteenth Amendment replaced the Eighth Amendment of 1985. The Thirteenth Amendment took away the powers of the President [Article 58 (2) (b)] to dissolve the national and provincial assemblies. Besides, the Fourteenth Amendment was passed on July 1 1997, also known as the Anti-Defection Bill, which aimed at checking floor crossing by parties and blackmailing leaders for personal gains. In a significant move, Nawaz backed the appointment of Mohammad Rafiq Tarar, a senator from Punjab, and former judge of the Supreme Court, as the President on January 1, 1999.[18]

The Fourth Blow (1999)

Three major events made Nawaz Sharif's tenure gain international attention—the nuclear explosions of May 28, 1998, the Lahore Declaration of February 21, 1999, and the Kargil War. The differences between Nawaz Sharif and General Pervez Musharraf came to the forefront over the Lahore Declaration that was signed on February 21, 1999, and the Military was uncomfortable with the rapprochement which was underway between India and Pakistan.

The fundamentalist parties, especially the Jamaat-e-Islami, were resentful of Atal Behari Vajpayee's historic visit and the Lahore Declaration, and organized massive demonstrations across the country primarily in Punjab. It was later known that while the Lahore Agreement was being signed, the Military was busy giving final touches to its Kargil misadventure.

Since 1988, while the political forces were incessantly scoring points against each other to the detriment of democracy, the Military kept a close watch on the political tussle between Nawaz Sharif and Benazir Bhutto. The Military was not only annoyed with the rapprochement efforts between India and Pakistan, it was also quite upset with the manipulations of Nawaz Sharif to engineer a split in the top Military echelons. Nawaz's move to appoint Lt. General Ziauddin as the ISI chief had alienated the Military, more so Musharraf, without whose consultation the appointment was made. With the war in Kargil already underway, the tussle between Nawaz Sharif and Pervez Musharraf reached breaking point when Nawaz Sharif along with his brother and the ISI chief went to the US to persuade the US President to pressurize the Military to withdraw from Kargil.

The countdown for Nawaz Sharif started when he sacked General Musharraf in absentia (who was on his way back from an official visit to Sri Lanka) and appointed Lieutenant General Khwaza Ziauddin Ahmed as the new COAS. It is believed that General Aziz, a trusted aide of Musharraf, who had sensed the crisis in making, worked out the modalities of the coup, for his master. He first ensured that Musharraf's aircraft was allowed the permission to land. After his arrival Musharraf took charge and with impeccable swiftness the coup was finally executed on the evening of October 12, 1999. Nawaz Sharif, his brother Shahbaz, and General Ziauddin were put into 'protective custody' and the National Assembly and provincial assemblies stood dissolved. A state of Emergency was declared and Musharraf assumed charge as the Chief Executive (a new title for a Military dictator) of Pakistan.

The Drivers for Military Intervention

Military coups and Military's interference in domestic politics has been a common feature of the international system portraying the eternal tussle for power between the civil and Military, the two opposing interest groups in a State. In several instances elected governments have surrendered their autonomy to the Military and subsequently got toppled or agreed to function largely within the confines of the Military's directives. In South Asia, Pakistan has epitomised this classical rivalry spanning over several decades, prompting one to look into the factors and circumstances that gave birth to Praetorian ambitions among the senior ranking Military officers.

Literature on Military coup and intervention suggests that coups are reactive as well as pre-emptive in nature and there could be various factors that encourage the Military for such an adventurism. The factors could range from the failure of the civilian government's performance and the loss of its legitimacy to the Military's own resolve to guard its corporate interests such as adequate budgetary support, autonomy in managing their internal affairs, the preservation of their responsibilities in the wake of outside interference and the continuity of the institutions itself. The legitimacy factor is a key component of the Military's interventionist ambitions transforming into a *coup d'etat.*[19]

Just like any other institution the Military also has its own interests which it guards at all occasions. The Military's interests or its corporate interests so to say, are vital for it to sustain as a credible force and institution. Any threat or incursion in the Military's domain, which may harm its corporate interests, makes a strong case for Military's intervention to restore the status quo.[20] Ayesha Siddiqa, a long time watcher of Pakistani Military affairs asserts, "The Military as a serious economic actor which competes with other domestic economic players, is a phenomenon prevalent primarily in the developing world, especially in countries ridden with the problem of political underdevelopment... In weak polities in particular, militaries are tempted to engage in economic ventures for a number of reasons, ranging from the welfare of their own personnel to filling the financial gap in order to meet their operational and personnel needs—especially when the governments cannot do so due to a resource crunch, or because the state has a poor tax base that does not allow it to generate resources—or merely to fulfill certain other objectives of the state."[21] The Military does not appreciate any kind of slashing in the defence budget ordered by the civilian government for want of other developmental priorities. In Pakistan, the 'Indian threat' on the eastern front and the instability in Afghanistan on the western front called for a strong and modernized Army. Hence no civilian government could afford to reduce the defence spending which suggests that safeguarding against any likely slashing of the defence budget was never a catalyst for all of Military coups in Pakistan.

A careful analysis would show that the reasons prompting Pakistan's Military to capture power rested in the policies of the civilian governments to interfere with the internal matters of the Military pertaining to appointments, promotions, tenure and ranks of the officers; and the failure and loss of legitimacy on part of the civilian governments due to misgovernance, political chaos and corruption. The measures introduced by Zulfiqar Ali Bhutto, such as the creation of the Frontier Security Force; introduction of Article 6 and 245 to check Military coups; change in the command structure; and the abolishing of the post of Commander-in-Chief (C-in-C) alienated the Military which took them as a blatant attack on its autonomy. At all moments in Pakistan's democratic history it was an established fact that the Prime Minister happened to be the weakest force in the *Troika* of the President, Army Chief and Prime Minister. The confrontation between the Prime Minister and the President happened to be a proxy war between the Army Chief and the Prime Minister. If one looks at the repeated overthrow of the civilian regimes between 1988-1999, one would find the tussle over the selection and appointment of the service chiefs has always been a common factor at the core of the downfall of civilian governments. In the overthrow of Benazir Bhutto's 1988-1990 reign, among other issues retirement of Admiral Iftikhar Ahmed Sirohey, who was also the chairman of the Joint Chief of Staff Committee (JCSC), severely damaged her relations with not only President Ghulam Ishaq Khan but also with the Military's top brass.[22] Likewise, during Nawaz Sharif tenure (1990-1993) discord with President Ghulam Ishaq Khan had surfaced over who would succeed General Mirza Aslam Beg following untimely death of General Asif Nawaz Janjua in January 1993.[23] When Benazir

Bhutto returned to power in 1993, this time, she locked horns with President Farooq Leghari over the selection of the successor of General Abdul Waheed.[24] Similarly, the catalyst for Nawaz Sharif's overthrow in 1999 happened to be his decision to sack General Musharraf in absentia (he was on an official visit to Sri Lanka) and appoint Director General, Inter Services Intelligence (ISI) Lieutenant General Khwaza Ziauddin as the new COAS.

Noted scholar Hasan Askari Rizvi identifies six key concerns of the Military — national security (nuclear weapons), overseas weapons and equipment procurement, autonomy from civilian interference, requisite defence expenditure, use of power and martial law, and socio-political stability. According to Rizvi, the Military is overtly averse to any compromise on Pakistan's core concerns and therefore is opposed to Indo-Pakistan rapprochement under civilian rule; particularly at the cost of the Kashmir issue and nuclear weapons. This explains why the Military has always kept Pakistan's Kashmir and nuclear weapons programme under its strict control. It zealously guards against any civilian interference in overseas weapons and equipment procurements, primarily because it believes that no other entity would understand better the rationale for such procurements. It has no qualms with discussion over defence expenditure with the civilian authorities but would not approve of any slashing of it just to keep its perks and privileges intact. Any sort of civilian interference with the services' structures and internal workings is totally unacceptable to the Military which becomes self-evident in the overthrows of various civilian governments over the years.[25] In addition, a glance over the period since 1958 till the 1999 coup would reveal that the military has always concocted the failure of civilian authorities and regimes in maintaining law and order, political stability, checking corruption and thus threatening 'national security', to take over. When General Ayub Khan took charge, establishing the first Military regime in the history of Pakistan, on October 27, 1958, he forced President Iskander Mirza to silently resign enabling the first Military takeover to materialize without a single shot being fired. It is not difficult to sense an utter contempt and dislike which Ayub Khan carried against the politicians, in his address of October 8, 1958. The entire speech rested on taking a higher moral ground by claiming that the armed forces had no distinct interest in politics but had to act against the failings of the politicians that had made the country a 'laughing stock'. He even cited his rejection of several offers by President Ghulam Ahmed to take over which could not be substantiated as Ghulam Ahmed had passed away before he made this speech. Nonetheless, misrule, corruption, mis-governance and political rivalry seemed to be the major factors that 'compelled' Ayub Khan to take such a 'drastic and extreme step'. The following key excerpts from General Ayub Khan's address would help understand the above explanations better.

> *"...This (martial law) is a drastic and extreme step taken with great reluctance, but with the fullest conviction that there was no alternative to it except the disintegration and complete ruination of the country..."*

> *"...These chaotic conditions, as you know have been brought about by self seekers who, in the garb of political leaders, have ravaged the country or tried to barter it away for personal gains..."*

> *"...Ever since the death of Qaid-e-Azam and Mr. Liaquat Ali Khan, politicians started a free-for-all type of fighting in which no holds were barred. They waged ceaseless and bitter war against each other, regardless of the ill-effect on the country, just whet their appetites and satisfy their base motive. There has been no limit to the depth of their baseness, chicanery, deceit and degradation. Having nothing constructive to offer, they used provincial feelings, sectarian, religious and racial differences to set a Pakistani against a Pakistani. They could see no good in anybody else. In this mad rush for power and acquisition all that mattered was self-interest. The country and people could go to the dogs as far as they were concerned. There were a few honourable exceptions but their conscience was dead and they were rendered ineffective by hordes of their supporters in the*

Assemblies changing party affiliation from day to day..."

"...In the process, all ideals and the high sense of values inherent in our religion and culture have been destroyed. The result is total administrative, economic, political and moral chaos in the country, which cannot be tolerated in these dangerous times..."

> *"... We solemnly decided to build a true national Army free from politics, a model of devotion to duty and integrity imbued with the spirit of service to the people and capable of effectively defending the country..."*

> *"...You may not know, but I refused on several occasions the late Mr. Ghulam Mohammad's offer to take over the country. I did so in the belief that I could serve the cause of Pakistan better from the place where I was, and also had a faint hope that some politicians would rise to the occasion and lead the country to a better future. Events have falsified those hopes and we have come to the present pass..."*[26]

Ironically, the long list of charges which Ayub Khan mentioned in his speech that compelled him to stage the coup was very much present in the letter (read resignation) which he handed over to General Yahya Khan, C-in-C on March 24, 1969. In his letter he accepted his failure in not being able to fix all those problems which a decade ago had spurred him to establish the first Military regime. The letter said:

> *"...It is with profound regret that I have come to the conclusion that all civil administration and constitutional authority in the country has become ineffective. If the situation continues to deteriorate at the present alarming rate, all economic life, indeed, civilized existence will become impossible..."*

> *"...The economic life of the country has all but collapsed. Workers and labourers are being incited and urged to commit acts of lawlessness and brutality. While demands*

> *for higher wages, salaries and amenities are being extracted under threat of violence, production in going down..."*
>
> *"...I have exhausted all possible civil and constitutional means to resolve the present crisis...The members of the Assembly are no longer free agents and there is no likelihood of the agreed two points being faithfully adopted. Indeed, members are being threatened and compelled either to boycott the session or to move such amendments as would liquidate the Central Government, make the maintenance of the Armed Forces impossible, divide the economy or the country and break up Pakistan into little bits and pieces..."*
>
> *"...It is beyond the capacity of the civil government to deal with the present complex situation, and the Defence Forces must step in..."*[27]

Later, on March 25, 1969, Ayub Khan in his last address in a rather pessimistic tone had observed:

> *"...It hurts me deeply to say that the situation now is no longer under the control of the Government. All Government institutions have become victim of coercion, fear and intimidation..."*
>
> *"Every principle, restraint and way of civilized existence has been abandoned. Every problem of the country is being decided in the streets. Except for the Armed Forces there is no constitutional and effective way to meet the situation. The whole nation demands that General Yahya Khan, the Commander-in-Chief of the Pakistan Army should fulfill his constitutional responsibilities..."*[28]

General Ayub Khan's letter and address to the nation revealed his regime's allegiance to the armed forces and even during his rule as constitutional President he regarded the Military as the saviour of Pakistan's destiny. His request to Yahya Khan that "the armed forces must step in" exposed the dichotomy in his political philosophy and established that his regime was not completely run and controlled by the Military, both in technical and the absolute sense. He prepared the ground for Yahya Khan to take over, confirming that even after his retirement in 1960 from active service and ten years of subsequent constitutional presidency, Ayub Khan remained a loyal soldier to the core. It goes to show the strong fraternity that runs within the Military and the desire among the serving and retired officers alike to uphold its interests at all occasions.

The Military also remained alert to exploit and even stoke public discontent against civilian governments on various counts. In 1969 Yahya Khan is believed to have stoked public unrest against the regime of Ayub Khan, who notwithstanding his military background was seen to be technically heading a civilian regime. General Yahya Khan on his part smoothly took over by using Ayub Khan's request to take over on the one hand and citing widespread unrest which was being spearheaded by his trusted aide Zulfiqar Ali Bhutto, on the other. Across Pakistan Zulfiqar Ali Bhutto was galvanizing a democratic movement after the establishment of his Pakistan People's Party in 1967. Yahya Khan proclaimed:

> "*...You have already heard Field Marshal Mohammad Ayub Khan's speech, which was broadcast on Tuesday and by now, you must also have read his letter of 24 March...*"

> "*...As proclaimed earlier I have imposed Martial Law throughout Pakistan...the situation has deteriorated to such an extent that normal law enforcing methods have become totally ineffective and have almost completely broken down. Serious damage to life and property has occurred and state of panic has paralysed life in the nation. Production has gone down to a dangerously low level, and economy generally has suffered an unprecedented setback. Strikes and violence have become a daily routine and the country has been driven to the edge of an abyss. The nation has to be pulled back to safety and normal conditions have to be restored without delay. The armed forces could not remain idle spectators of*

> *this state of near anarchy. They have to do their duty and save the country from utter disaster. I have, therefore, taken this step..."*[29]

Likewise, in his address General Zia-ul Haq had cited political instability due to PPP-PNA tussle as the primary reason for the coup. He said:

> *"...I genuinely feel that the survival of this country lies in democracy and democracy alone. It is mainly due to this belief that Armed Forces resisted the temptation to take over during the recent provocative circumstances in spite of diverse massive political pressures..."*

> *"...we hoped that this climate of agitational frenzy came to an end, the nation would be able to appreciate the correct and constitutional role of the Armed Forces and all fears would be allayed...It must be quite clear to you now that when the political leaders failed to steer the country out of a crisis, it is an inexcusable sin for the Armed Forces to sit as silent spectators..."*

> *"...I would like to point out here that I saw no prospects of a compromise between the People's Party and the PNA, because their mutual distrust and lack of faith. It was feared that the PNA and PPP to reach a compromise would throw the country into chaos and the country would thus be plunged into a more serious crisis. The risk could not be taken in the larger interest of the country..."*[30]

After an eleven year rule, General Zia died in an air crash in 1988 and military was out of direct rule for eleven years. This decade of democracy was characterized by the Military interfering in decision making and controlling the Executive from behind the scenes and both Benazir Bhutto and Nawaz Sharif assuming charge twice, but failing to complete their full term on both the occasions.

On October 12, 1999, the popularly elected government of

Nawaz Sharif was overthrown by General Pervez Musharraf, who took over as the Chief Executive of Pakistan. It seems he consciously chose the title of Chief Martial Law Administrator to convey that it was not a pure martial law and the armed forces would not stay in power for any longer than necessary. Domestically, he was at ease due to the capabilities of his forces to remain in control and lack of political opposition which on the contrary appeared justifying Nawaz Sharif's ouster. The public offered no protest either and celebrated with drums and sweets on the streets, such was the level of antipathy towards Nawaz Sharif's regime.

Taking a cue from his predecessors General Musharraf without any delay addressed the nation in the wee hours of October 13, 1999, at 2:45 a.m. He proclaimed:

> *"You are all aware of the kind of turmoil and uncertainty that our country has gone through in recent times. Not only have all the institutions been played around with and systematically destroyed, the economy too is in a state of collapse... The armed forces have been facing incessant public clamour to remedy the fast declining situation from all sides of the political divide..."*
>
> *"...All my efforts and counsel to the Government, it seems, were to no avail. Instead they now turned their attention on the Army itself. Despite all my advices, they tried to interfere with the armed forces, the last remaining viable institution in which all of you take so much pride and look up to, at all times, for the stability, unity and integrity of our beloved country. Our concerns again were conveyed in no uncertain terms, but the Government of Mr. Nawaz Sharif chose to ignore all these, and tried to politicize the Army, destabilize it and tried to create dissension within its ranks..."*
>
> *"...I was in Sri Lanka on an official visit. On my way back, the PIA commercial flight was not allowed to*

> *land at Karachi, but was ordered to be diverted to anywhere outside Pakistan, despite acute shortage of fuel, imperiling the life of all the passengers. Thanks be to Allah, this evil design was thwarted through speedy Army action..."*
>
> *"...My dear countrymen, having briefly explained the background, I wish to inform you that the armed forces have moved in as a last resort, to prevent any further destabilization..."*

General Musharraf's has been by far the shortest of all maiden addresses given by the Military dictators following the coup which indicates the unplanned nature of the coup. The situation was very tense and fluid and he first needed to tighten any possible loose ends by deploying his troops at key places such as the Parliament, Supreme Court, houses of top political leaders and government installations. Once assured of his control across the country he proceeded with his address which had to be written at a short notice and thus lacked comprehensiveness in terms of articulation of the justification for his actions. The sheer length of the addresses by Ayub Khan and Zia-ul-Haq suggests that they have been planning the coup for long and hence had readymade draft to be delivered with some additional inputs related to immediate events preceding the coup. In his October 13 address, towards the end, General Musharraf said that he did not wish to make any lengthy policy statement because as a matter of fact he had none at that time. Only in his next address on October 17, did he give a detailed description of the prevailing state of affairs, challenges that his Military regime and Pakistan confronted and what he intended to do. He covered all aspects under the sun including law and order; social, sectarian and economic challenges, accountability, governance, nation-building and foreign policy, among others at length.

In all the addresses by coup leaders one can notice a set pattern of charges such as the failings of the political leaders, economic collapse, internal disorder and failure of civilian and constitutional authority, among others. General Musharraf too, in his short address of October 12, cited the destruction of institutions by politicians and civilian interference in military's internal affairs as the drivers for his coup. The decade of democracy between 1988 and 1999 would show that the Military did not appreciate the interference of Benazir Bhutto and Nawaz Sharif with the appointment of service chiefs during their rules. In that period, the Military simply pressurized the President to sack the governments which were seen to be working against its interest while avoiding any blame on itself. In one instance, in 1993 the Military had got both President Ghulam Ishaq Khan and Prime Minister Nawaz Sharif to resign in a compromise solution over a range of issues—dispute over the appointment of the Army Chief, the Gulf War, the *Sharia* bill and Nawaz Sharif's independent initiatives towards Afghanistan and Kashmir. What also seemed to have annoyed the President was the government's decision to scrap the Eighth Amendment and not to back him for another term. In the end, it was a master stroke by the then Army Chief General Asif Nawaz Janjua which not only re-affirmed the clout of the COAS but also the overarching influence of the Military in political affairs.

Another contradicting facet of the addresses by the Army Chiefs has been that while they cited the failure of democratic institutions and politicians in providing effective governance as reason for their actions they, in the same breadth, emphasized the indispensability of democracy for Pakistan as the ideal form of government and that it would be restored soon. However, this should not be construed as the Military's keenness for a democratic rule as it was only meant to hoodwink the people and the international community. As Pakistan would witness under different military rules, such rhetorical proclamations soon got lost in the barrage of anti-democratic legislations and measures. Constitutions were tailored and tampered with, institutions were destroyed, freedom of all types was curtailed and unconstitutional means were adopted by the Army Chiefs to hold on to political power.

Military's Modus Operandi

Pakistan's Military has always been at the centre stage of the country's nation-building process, be it dealing with internal troubles or facing external threats. After the death of Muhammad Ali Jinnah and Liaquat Ali Khan there was no charismatic leader who could have shaped democratic institution-building. The Military, with the induction of Ayub Khan in the government, was brought into the mainstream, when the Constitution was still not drafted. Thus, the Military placed itself to exploit the weak civilian leadership and define its political role through Constitutions, which favoured the Military's active participation in political affairs.

In the initial phase, the Army played a more civilian role of dealing with the natural disasters, rehabilitation of the refugees, communal riots and food shortages. Its political ambition germinated with Ayub Khan's ascendancy to power. During this phase, the Army dominated State affairs with the support of the bureaucracy. Along with Ayub Khan, Ghulam Muhammad, Chaudhary Muhammad Ali and Iskander Mirza ran the affairs of the State. With a supportive bureaucracy and a strong feudal class, the Army took advantage of the lack of political authority at the federal and provincial levels. As the top arbiters of country it took care of the interests of the bureaucracy. After 1958, the Military started relying more on the strong feudal class for implementing Ayub's 'basic democracy' system. Ayub throughout his rule depended on the bureaucracy because he had high faith in the experience and ability of the civilian bureaucracy, which comprised of highly competent and professional administrators.[31]

In 1971, after suffering a decisive and shattering defeat at India's hands, the Military withdrew from active politics but remained vital in the overall scheme of the government until 1977. During Zulfiqar Ali Bhutto's rule between 1971-1977, it was instrumental in maintaining law and order, when Martial Law was imposed in Hyderabad, Karachi and Lahore. This indispensability of the Military in domestic affairs kept nurturing the ambitions of the generals to regain State power.

General Zia-ul-Haq on his part followed a six-pronged strategy to control the power structures of Pakistan. First, he consciously built his reputation as a devout muslim commander. Second, he nursed his relationship with the Ulema and religious parties, such as Jamaat-e-Islami to raise a civilian workforce which would not only propagate and enforce his Islamic policies but also counter the democratic parties, primarily the PPP. Third, he embarked on a massive Islamization drive through political, judicial and academic means. Fourth, the execution of Zulfiqar Ali Bhutto gave a strong message to the democratic forces in Pakistan about his ruthlessness and determination to establish a militarized Pakistan against all odds. Fifth, after the Soviet invasion of Afghanistan in 1979, with US financial support, Zia on the one hand aroused apprehensions within the Islamic countries about the Soviet occupation in Afghanistan, and on the other, launched a massive madarassa creation drive to produce a staunch Army of Mujahideens in the name of jihad. Islam had become his most trusted and powerful weapon for power aggrandizement. Lastly, he always kept an 'Indian threat' alive to argue for Military's indispensability for Pakistan's security and survival. His support to terrorism in Punjab, in tandem, was meant to keep the ante up with India.[32]

The Army has always maintained a strong correlation between internal security and foreign policy challenges and maintained the centrality of its role and rule in meeting both ends. They have successfully exploited an 'Indian threat' to their advantage in developing a strong Military which ironically was used more in serving the purpose of US interests in the region. Since the 1950s, Pakistan's strategic relationship with the US and its decision to join the South East Asia Treaty Organization (SEATO) and Central Treaty Organization (CENTO) enabled it to secure US economic and military assistance and help enhance build its capabilities. Analysts believe that Pakistan's relationship with the US and China has invariably been a key factor in promoting Military's adventurism by Pakistan by illuminating its adversarial relationship with India, which was evident in 1965 and 1971, and the proxy war since 1984 and the Kargil War in 1999.[33]

The role of Army dictators has not remained confined to only building Pakistan's Military prowess but has also encompassed multiple roles ranging from drafting the Constitution, through policing and policy planning to formulating foreign and security policies. It has enjoyed effective control over the functioning of the civilian governments and pulled strings from behind the curtain while out of active politics. The impregnability of the Army's command and control over Pakistan and the lethal clout of its affiliated arm in the Inter-Service Intelligence (ISI) convinced the political players of all shades to respect its power and keep good relations if not ally with it. Some analysts offer a very interesting and unique explanation of the Army's success in Pakistan. Mushahid Hussain and Akmal Hussain observe, "In the Military, unlike the civilian bureaucracy, the officer has to study, acquire new skills and pass an examination at each stage of the promotion ladder. Over the last forty years the Military has developed a sophisticated infrastructure of education from Military public schools, through specialized colleges for professional training in various fields of engineering, electronics and aeronautics, to high quality command and staff training institutions."[34]

The Military intervention in Pakistan is a mixture of 'designed' as well as 'reactive militarism'. The system under Military rule could be called 'constitutional autocracy', 'Military oligarchy' and 'preventive autocracy'.[35] Despite Nawaz Sharif's landslide victory in 1997, the democratic forces could not provide any match for the Military's professional capabilities. The inability of the democratic forces to stand up to the might of the Military generals was also due to the inept and corrupt governments that were headed by Nawaz Sharif and Benazir Bhutto between 1998 and 1999. The erosion of public faith in the governance of the democratic regimes, allegedly due to rampant corruption, gave the Military a pretext to stage coups in Pakistan to the peoples' delight. Nonetheless, it was unfortunate for democracy and Pakistan to have witnessed people celebrate the overthrow of the popularly elected Nawaz Sharif government with drums and sweets. A little boy, who was with General Musharraf on the same flight, which was refused permission to land, reportedly said, "I and my family are glad that General Musharraf is in charge of Pakistan now and are sure he will prove to be a good leader."[36] The autocratic ways of Nawaz Sharif and never-ending craving for wealth and power eroded the support of the opposition parties and leaders, who are also to blame for not being able to rise above their personal vendetta in the larger interest of democracy. Benazir Bhutto and Qazi Hussain Ahmed, the chief of Jamaat-e-Islami (JI) were among many others who expressed relief over Nawaz Sharif's ouster which showed a gradual decline in democratic solidarity and principles during the ten years of personal and political vendetta. Parties meekly watched the Military onslaught on the political system's edifice, forgetting that they were themselves major stakeholders in it.[37]

After the coup in 1999, General Musharraf geared himself to restore the inevitable position in which the Military had always found itself. He strengthened Military's role by consolidating his own position in a time-tested fashion. Taking a cue from Ayub Khan and Zia-ul Haq, he held a Presidential Referendum on April 30, 2002 to oxygenate himself for another five-year term. The Referendum, largely deemed as unconstitutional exposed General Musharraf's hidden scheme to consolidate powers in his hands and legitimize Military's re-entry into mainstream politics for many years to come. Ironically, Qazi Hussain Ahmed who had expressed satisfaction over the ouster of Sharif in 1999 was the first to cry foul and challenged the Referendum in the court.[38] Likewise, other parties, who had tacitly endorsed Musharraf's coup were now arguing that there was no provision in the Constitution for holding Referendum for the office of President.[39] Understanding the inherent nature of party politics wherein deceit and backstabbing were very much accepted practices, Musharraf utterly disregarded the utterances and criticisms of the opposition. To soothe international and domestic criticisms Musharraf began to introduce 'guided democracy' to the Military's advantage. He crippled the leading political parties, PPPP and PML-N by expelling their leaders Benazir Bhutto and Nawaz Sharif out of country and created a new party consisting of PPPP and PML-N deserters and floor crossers. The creation of PML-Q (Quaid-e-Azam), also referred to as the 'King's party' was done at Musharraf's command. Similarly, the meteoric rise of Islamist parties under a unified banner, the MMA, too, was facilitated by Musharraf to a large extent. Both these parties were to play a sheet anchor role in erecting a façade of 'democracy' in the following years to hoodwink critics of the authoritarianism.

The October 2002 elections saw PML-Q with 115, PPPP[40] with 80, MMA with 58, PML-N (Nawaz) with 19, Muttahida Qaumi

Movement (MQM) with 17 and National Alliance (NA) with 14 seats in the National Assembly.[41] The MMA secured an absolute majority in the North West Frontier Province (NWFP) and formed the government in Balochistan as well.

However, the opposition continued rallying support against Musharraf and his puppet regime and paralyzing the National Assembly on the issue of Legal Framework Order (LFO) of 1999, National Security Council (NSC), and the one-man-one-post issue. The MMA which was a beneficiary of Musharraf's machinations also made life difficult for Musharraf to a large extent through its opposition to Musharraf's pro-US policies and LFO but that did not prevent the opposition from accusing the MMA of betraying the Alliance for the Restoration for Democracy (ARD) in the fight against Military rule.

In July 2004, in an interesting and politically significant development, General Musharraf masterminded another leadership change, this time rather smoothly and without any major controversy. Prime Minister Zafarullah Jamali was asked to resign and was replaced by Chaudhary Shujaat Hussain, president of PML-Q as a stopgap arrangement and Finance Minister Shaukat Aziz was declared Prime Minister-elect. Shaukat Aziz needed to win a seat for himself in the National Assembly to become eligible for premiership. Shaukat Aziz filed nominations from Attock in Punjab and Tharparkar in Sindh. Elections were held on August 18 and Shaukat Aziz won both the seats with huge margins and was elected as Prime Minister on August 25, 2004.[42] The peaceful manner in which the change in leadership was executed, it should be considered Musharraf's contribution to Pakistan's democratic system. He set a precedent where the Military need not take the extreme step of overthrowing the entire government through Article 58 (2)(b) when the purpose could be served by merely replacing the Prime Minister. The Editorial in *The Herald* wrote, "Prime Minister Zafarullah Khan Jamali's ouster on June 26 was described as the smoothest transfer of power in the country's history... Sycophants who seem to have flocked to General Musharraf's camp in great numbers in recent times would go even to the extent of arguing that the 'smooth' transfer of power reflects the maturity of the political system engineered by the Army Chief over the last five years. Who needs Article 58-2(b) anyway?"[43] This can be seen as General Musharraf's original contribution to guided democracy in Pakistan, something that was perhaps never attempted by his predecessors.

Military's Corporate Muscle

Drawing parallel with British colonialism, in which the British acquired large tracts of land for setting up Military cantonments, Military farms, laying railway lines for ensuring better control and revenue extraction, analysts find Pakistan's Military following a similar strategy popularly referred to as 'cantonment colonialism'. The Military is seen as a new colonizer and under the new colonial framework cantonments have become new metropolis' and the civilians have been relegated to the status of 'natives'. The COAS is seen as the modern-day viceroy, reigning supreme and only answerable to Washington as the British Viceroy was to London.[44] The Military today is the largest and richest corporate house and landowner in Pakistan which includes scores of industries, trading houses, banking, leasing and insurance companies, transport corporations, and real and housing estates. The Fauji Foundation and Army Welfare Trust run about 55 industrial and commercial enterprises whereas the National Logistics Cell is believed to be controlling road transport cargo movements. Critics see Pakistan as a Praetorian State with a 'softening national state apparatus wherein private interests takes precedence over state interest'. In other words, when Military officers, after being trained for warfare, begin to manage real estate, water supply systems, steel mills, and fertilizer factories, their fundamental training goes waste in terms of resources, time and effort. The debate, therefore, is that whether Military officials are capable or efficient enough to handle activities and tasks they are not trained for. There is a school of thought that believes that a Praetorian State is a contradiction in terms of the objectives of developing a modern State in a globalised economy.[45] Ayesha Siddiqa writes: "The Pakistani

Military is among the several other armed forces in the world engaged in commercial ventures. Today, its financial empire has an approximate financial size of 200 billion rupees with Military-controlled welfare foundations operating in areas ranging from banking, insurance, leasing and real estate to private security, education, airlines, cargo services, knitwear, and major agro-based industries".[46] Hasan Askari Rizvi observed, "The Military under General Musharraf has undergone a major transformation, particularly in the outlook of the top commanders. They are no longer satisfied with the protection and advancement of their professional and corporate interests from the sidelines. The Military has expanded its non-professional interests to such an extent that it has developed stakes in most areas of policy making and management".[47] There is no dearth of writings on Military's corporate undertakings and business conglomerates in Pakistan. In the October 2004 issue of *Newsline,* Zahid Hussain has written that since 1999 General Musharraf's regime has placed 1,200 active and retired officers in various ministries and state corporations and retired generals have been made vice-chancellors of universities and heads of think tanks. Five foundations including Fauji Foundation, the Army Welfare Trust, Shaheen Foundation and Bahria Foundation controlled by the Military are regarded as the largest business groups in Pakistan. These foundations are running banks, insurance, fertilizers and cement companies, owning agricultural farms, dairies and gas stations and are heavily into land-grabbing for Defence Societies. In Lahore, more than 100 square miles of land starting from Burki road to the BRB canal and across has been acquired and in other big cities like Karachi, the situation is no different. In fact, as per some estimates around 35 per cent of Karachi's prime land is under the cantonment board, which makes even retired Military officials such as Lieutenant General (Retd.) Talat Masood call it "institutionalized corruption".[48]

In the same issue of *Newsline*, there is a long list of organizations where the armed forces personnel are serving at top positions. These include the Karachi Electricity Supply Corporation, the Karachi Port Trust, the National Transport Research Centre, the Pakistan Ordinance Factories, Pakistan Rangers, Pakistan Steel, PTCL, the Afghan Refugees Organization, the Airport Security Force, the Capital

Development Authority—Islamabad, the Carrier Telephone Industry, the Civil Aviation Authority, the Commerce Ministry, the Defence Division, the Defence Production Division, the Establishment Division, the Evacuee Trust Property Board, the Federal Employees Benevolent Fund, the Federal Public Services Commission, the Finance Division, the Gwadar Port Authority, the Intelligence Bureau, the Interior Division, the IT & Telecom Division, the Labour Ministry's National Training Bureau, the Labour, Manpower & Overseas Pakistanis Division, the Military Lands & Cantonment Department, the Ministry of Culture, Sports, Tourism and Youth Affairs, the Ministry of Education, the Ministry of Food and Agriculture, the Ministry of Housing and Works, the Ministry of Industries and Production, the Ministry of Information, the Ministry of Petroleum & Natural Resources, the Ministry of water and Power, the Minorities Ministry, the Narcotics Control Division, the National Highway Authority, the National Highways & Motorways Police, the National Logistics Cell, the National Reconstruction Bureau (NRB), the Pakistan Armed Services Board, the Pakistan Marine Academy, the Pakistan Mineral Development Authority, the Pakistan Sports Board, the Pakistan Tourist Development Corporation, the Planning and Development Division, the President's Secretariat, the S&TR Division, the Women's Development and Special Education Ministries and Utility Stores Corporation of Pakistan (Pvt.) Ltd.[49]

Armed forces personnel apart from being omnipresent are also being given special salaries. In the NRB, a retired Brigadier is getting in the range of 1,40,000-1,50,000 rupees per month, a retired colonel is drawing 1,25,000 rupees, and a major around 50,000 rupees per month. Besides, barring a few corruption cases by the armed forces personnel is seldom made public unlike in the cases of their civilian counterparts. If at all any action is taken against armed forces personnel, it is done in secrecy. Various NAB reports suggest that the country has lost billions of dollars due to kickbacks to the Army Welfare Trust and Shaheen and Bahria Foundations in international defence deals pertaining to tanks, submarines, mine hunters, Mirage fighters and Army jeeps. Ironically, despite having substantial evidences, the NAB seems little inclined to initiate proceedings against the senior ranking officials including three former Army Chiefs, two

Naval Chiefs, and an Air Force Chief.[50]

Muhammad Aamir Mughal in a thought-provoking article presented a fairly long list of serving and retired Military officials inducted into different ministries and missions and ambassadorial assignments. Overall, the broad range of areas in which Military officials have been posted included communications, education, diplomacy, water and electricity management, information, post office, jails, local bodies, think tanks, industrial production, shipping, minority affairs, population welfare, health, agriculture, railways, highways, housing, labour and manpower, social and women's development, law and justice and sub-sectors of sports, including hockey and cricket. The article claimed that since General Musharraf's coup in October 1999 till 2002-2003, around 104 serving Lieutenant-Generals, Major-Generals or equivalent in other services were among 1,027 Military officials to have been sent on assignments in ministries, and Pakistani missions abroad. Plus, 160 officers of the rank of Brigadier and equivalent in other services were given assignments in similar areas. For instance, 13 in cabinet division, 5 in commerce ministry, 98 in communications ministry, 113 in the defence division, 52 in the defence production division, 9 in education ministry, 16 in the establishment division, 24 in the ministry of foreign affairs, 6 in the ministry of food, agriculture, and livestock, 88 in the interior ministry, 2 in the health ministry, 6 in the housing and works ministry, 29 in the industries and production ministry, 3 in the information and broadcasting ministry, 58 in ministry of information and technology, 25 in the Kashmir affairs and northern affairs ministry, 5 in the labour and manpower division, 17 in the ministry of minorities affairs, 39 in the ministry of petroleum and natural resources and one each in ministry of population and the planning and development division and the ministry of religious affairs. Besides, there are 2 Military officials in the revenue division (CBR), 21 in the ministry of science and technology, 72 in ministry of railways/ railway board, 37 in the ministry of water and power, 5 in the ministry of women's development, 6 in Wafaqi Mohtasib. Moreover, 37 more appointments have been made through the 10 per cent quota that the Military has in civilian posts across Pakistan.[51] Also, between

1999 and 2003, 13 Lieutenant-Generals and Major-Generals were sent as ambassadors to different missions around the world, whereas one Brigadier and Major too got ambassadorial postings.[52]

A glance through the names of some of the companies that the Military runs in Pakistan would show the range of business interest it possesses.[53] The list is as follows:

Institute of Management & Computer Science	1
College of education	1
Intermediate Colleges	2
Model Schools	81
Vocational Training Centres	67
Technical Training Centres	9
Referral Hospitals	6
Rural Hospitals	5
Fauji Foundation Medical Centres	24
Mobile Health Units	2
Dispensaries	27
Wards in Combined Military Hospitals (CMH)	1 (CMH Mardan)

Fauji Corn Complex, Jhengiria
Fauji Cereals, Rawalpindi
Foundation Gas, Rawalpindi
Fauji Metals, Rawalpindi
Fauji Polypropylene Products, Hub Chowki
Fauji Sugar Mills, Tando Muhammad Khan
Fauji Sugar Mills, Khoski
Fauji Sugar Mills, Sangla Hill
Fauji Foundation Experimental & Seed Multiplication farm, Nukerji, Sind
Fauji Software Company, Rawalpindi
Fauji Medical Transcription, Rawalpindi
Fauji Institute of Information and Technology & Medical Transcription
Fauji Oil Terminal Company, Karachi
NIC Project, Islamabad
Fauji Cement Company Ltd

Fauji Fertilizer Company Ltd
Fauji Jordan Company Ltd
Fauji Kabirwala Power Company Ltd
Mari Gas Company Ltd.

In Ayesha Siddiqa's words, "The armed forces' direct or indirect involvement in the economy and its parallel control of power politics allows it access to privileged information which, in Pakistan's case has allowed two welfare groups, the AWT, and the Fauji Foundation, to become two of the largest business conglomerates in the country. Besides access to strategic economic information, these business groups have been given tax breaks as well... A political Army's interest in remaining well-entrenched in politics become significant when it has equally significant financial stakes in staying on top of things."[54]

Conclusion

The primary role of the Military in Pakistan which was confined to merely securing the frontiers of the country against any external threat, gradually encompassed the responsibilities of dealing with domestic disturbances and law and order situations. To its advantage, the political elites committed a cardinal sin allowing a serving General in Ayub Khan to become the Defence Minister opened the gates for future generations of Generals to make further inroads. The inclusion of Military in politics was the end of the promise for democracy before it had barely taken roots in Pakistan. Slowly and steadily, as the Military started consolidating its power and standing through huge Military budgets in the name of countering the 'Indian threat', use of Islam and Ulema, tailoring of the Constitution to suit its interests, building corporate muscle and control of civilian offices, democratic functioning and roots in Pakistan began to weaken. Democratic and civil society institutions were not allowed to strengthen since they posed a challenge to the privileges which the Military enjoyed. The Soviet invasion of Afghanistan in 1979 meant more aid and support from the United States and till the present day, the General Headquarters (GHQ) draws sustenance from Washington. The United States' political and economic support to the Pakistan Military since the 1950s to further its own strategic interest in the region has strengthened the Military as an institution and at the expense of democracy in Pakistan. The manner in which General Musharraf has had his writ run in Pakistan following September 11, it seemed the US could not care less for democracy in Pakistan. Nawaz Sharif and Benazir Bhutto were exiled, the Constitution was tampered with yet again, political parties were intimidated and split to create a party loyal only to General Musharraf, and the religious parties were encouraged to counter PPPP and PML-N and support General Musharraf's political scheme. Despite the butchering that democracy has witnessed at the hands of the Military since 2002, concerns in the United States have been confined to Afghanistan and General Musharraf's role in the Global war against terrorism. Having been assured of his standing in Pakistan by the United States, General Musharraf consciously encroached into the corporate sector to enhance the Military's economic prowess. The appointment of senior Military officials at top positions in civilian offices and diplomatic missions suggests the long-term vision of the Military for Pakistan. Generals may come and go but the Military's influence in state affairs would remain unchallenged, even while they are sitting behind the curtains. Pakistan's Military has perfected the art of marginalizing democracy and promoting self-interest, and ironically the civilian forces, including the political parties and leaders, have played an important supportive role in the process. In this context, the next chapter dealing with the rise of the religious parties in Pakistan would show how the Military deliberately ensured their victory and reversal of mainstream political parties. This is one amongst the many strategies of the Military for shaping the destiny of Pakistan as per its own understanding and vision.

NOTES

1. Ian Talbot, *Pakistan: A Modern History*, Oxford University Press, New Delhi, 1998, p. 143.

2. Article 37 (6) of the Constitution said, "The Prime Minister shall hold office during the pleasure of the President, but the President shall not exercise his powers unless he is satisfied that the Prime Minister does not command the confidence of the majority of the members of the National Assembly". Hassan Abbas, *Poleaxe or Politics of the Eighth Amendment 1985-1997*. 1997. Watandost. Lahore, p. 34, p. 20.
3. Talbot, p. 127.
4. Ibid., pp. 154-155.
5. Ibid., pp. 154, 161.
6. Talbott, p. 195.
7. Hasan Askari Rizvi, *The Military and Politics in Pakistan 1947-86*, Konark Publishers, New Delhi, 1988, p. 180.
8. *Dawn*, 8 March 1971, cited in Rizvi, 1988, pp. 185-186.
9. Makdoom Ali Khan (ed.), *The Constitution of the Islamic Republic of Pakistan*, Pakistan Law House, 1989, p. 202.
10. Ibid., p. 7.
11. Hassan Abbas, *Poleaxe or Politics of the Eighth Amendment 1985-1997*, Watandost, Lahore, 1997, p. 34.
12. Ian Talbot, no. 1, pp. 233-242.
13. Ibid, p. 46.
14. Makdoom Ali Khan, 1989, p. 39-40.
15. Hassan Abbas, no. 2, p. 95.
16. Ayesha Jalal, *The State of Martial Rule: The Origins of Pakistan's Political Economy of Defence*, Cambridge University Press, Cambridge, 1990, p. 299, cited in Talbot 1998, p. 130.
17. Abbas, 1997, p. 17.
18. Story of Pakistan at http://www.storyofpakistan.com/timeline12.htm
19. Eric A. Nordlinger, Soldiers in Politics Military Coups and Governments, 1977, Prentice-Hall, New Jersey, p. 65.
20. Ibid., pp. 65-78.
21. Ayesha Siddiqa, "Soldiers of Fortune", *Newsline*, December 2006, p. 23.
22. Talbot, 1998, p. 309.
23. Ibid, p. 325.
24. Hassan Abbas no. 2, p. 101.

25. Hasan Askari Rizvi, "Civil Military Relations in Contemporary Pakistan", *Survival*, Vol. 40, No. 2, Summer 1998, pp. 96-113.
26. 'General (later Field Marshal) Ayub Khan's First Broadcast to the Nation: October 8, 1958' Appendix C, in Rizvi, 1988, pp. 275-278.
27. 'Text of the letter sent on March 24, 1969 by Field Marshal Ayub Khan to the C-in-C Pakistan Army, General Yahya Khan', Appendix D, in Hasan Askari Rizvi, 1988, pp. 279-281.
28. 'Field Marshal Ayub Khan's last address to the nation', March 25, 1969, Appendix E, in Hasan Askari Rizvi, 1988, p. 283
29. "General A.M. Yahya Khan's first broadcast to the nation", March 26, 1969", in Hasan Askari Rizvi, 1988, p. 285.
30. "General Muhammad Zia-ul Haq's first address to the Nation," July 5, 1977, Appendix H, in Hasan Askari Rizvi 1988, pp. 289-293.
31. Mushahid Hussain and Akmal Hussain, *Pakistan: Problem of Governance*. Konark Publishers; New Delhi. 1993, p. 19.
32. J.N. Dixit, *India-Pakistan in War and Peace*. Books Today; New Delhi. 2002, p. 248.
33. Veena Kukreja, *Contemporary Pakistan: Political Processes, Conflicts and Crises*, Sage Publications, New Delhi, 2003, p. 61.
34. Mushahid Hussain and Akmal Hussain, 1993, p. 15.
35. Nihal H. Rizvi, "Military Intervention in Pakistan", in Verinder Grover and Ranjana Arora (ed.) *Political System in Pakistan*, Deep and Deep Publications; New Delhi, 1995. pp. 25-38.
36. *The Herald*, November 1999, in Military Coup in Pakistan—A Selection of Articles, *Strategic Digest*. December 1999, p. 1790.
37. Zafar Abbas, Full Circle, The Herald, November 1999, *Strategic Digest*, December 1999, p. 1793.
38. B. Murlidhar Reddy, "Musharraf's Case Hearing on April 22". *The Hindu*, New Delhi, April 17, 2002.
39. "PML Launches Drive Against Referendum" at http://www.dawn.com/2002/04/13/nat3.htm.
40. There was a change in the nomenclature and *Parliamentarian* was suffixed to PPP to avoid disqualification from contesting the elections.
41. Case in Point, *The Herald*, December 2002, p. 20.
42. "Aziz Wins Both Seats by Huge Margins", at http://

www.dawn.com/2004/08/19/top1.htm

43. "A New Kind of Politics". *The Herald,* July 2004, p. 14.
44. Kaiser Bengali, "Perils of Militarised Politics", Pakistan People's Party website at *http://www.ppp.org.pk/dfc/kaiserbengali.html.* Originally published at http://www.dawn.com/2006/08/03/op.htm#1
45. Ibid.
46. Ayesha Siddiqa, 2006, p. 19.
47. Zahid Hussain, "A Military State", *Newsline,* October 2004, p. 28.
48. *Ibid.*
49. Massoud Ansari, "The Numbers Game", *Newsline,* October 2004, p. 31.
50. Massoud Ansari, "The Militarization of Pakistan", *Newsline,* October 2004, p. 31.
51. Muhammad Aamir Mughal, "Unemployment in Pakistan & Army-2", at *http://www.forum.atimes.com/topic.asp*? Topic_ID= 982, posted on 03'29/2005.
52. For a detailed list of Military officials with ranks and what assignments were they given inside Pakistan and aboard please see Muhammad Aamir Mughal's article (2005).
53. Aasim Sajjad Akhtar, "Fauji's Foundation", *Himal,* 16/11, November 2003, p. 45.
54. Ayesha Siddiqa, 2006, p. 20.

CHAPTER II

The Second Extreme

Rise and Rumblings of the Islamists

Since Pakistan's birth in 1947, the Islamist parties in Pakistan have managed to keep themselves in the mainstream through their clever use of religion, a successful projection of themselves as the rightful representatives of Islam and alliance with the civil-military oligarchy. They have been an important component of Pakistan's identity search and policies towards Afghanistan, India and the religious minorities within Pakistan. The Islamist parties increased their clout in Pakistan as more and more regimes, be it military or civilian, aligned with them to seek religious legitimacy, draw on their advise to make laws conforming to Islamic principles and counter nationalist and political opponents. Having said this, it is also true that in spite of their religious clout they failed to secure more than 18 seats in the National Assembly ever, without the establishment's support. Doubts still remain over their ability to secure over 20 seats on their own. Yet they cannot be brushed aside as an insignificant entity, for they do possess the potential to impact developments inside and outside Pakistan. With their unprecedented electoral victory in 2002, they have become a much more formidable force in Pakistan than ever before. This chapter looks into different factors and circumstances that may have facilitated their meteoric rise and helps understand their political prospects in the coming years.

2002 General Elections

Under the directives of the Supreme Court, general elections were to be held within three years of the October 1999 coup. The October 2002 elections can be termed as an election which saw no codes of conduct or rules being followed apart from those prescribed by the military, because on the results hinged the political survival of General Pervez Musharraf. The most noteworthy aspect of the elections, apart from the creation of the King's party or the Pakistan Muslim League Quaid-e-Azam (PML-Q), a mastermind of General Musharraf, was the unprecedented victory of a six-party alliance named the Muttahida Majlis-e-Amal (MMA). The MMA secured over 50 seats in the National Assembly, an absolute majority in the North West Frontier Province (NWFP) and second largest seats in Balochistan. Although in the National Assembly, the MMA ranked third behind the Pakistan Muslim League-Quaid-e-Azam (PML-Q) and the Pakistan People Party Parliamentarians (PPPP), it created history by wining so many seats in the National Assembly. In the previous elections, the highest number of seats that Islamist parties could win was 18 in the 1970 elections which makes the MMA's 2002 feat unprecedented and unparalleled, in Pakistan's democratic experience.

The 2002 elections were held under the vigilant and strict supervision of General President Pervez Musharraf. The elections witnessed a rather unimpressive performance by the PPPP and PML-Q partially due to faults of their own making and due to the establishment's deliberate marginalization policies. It also saw a new political entity—the PML-Q being added to the long tally of national parties. A product of Musharraf's political machinations, the PML-Q was popularly referred to as the King's party, for obvious reasons.

However, going by the historical precedents in Pakistan wherein the army and the mullahs collaborated for electoral and extra-electoral purposes, the success of the MMA simply reinforced historic liaisons. An analysis of the pre-election positioning by General Musharraf and the impact of other contemporary developments help explain the rise of MMA. In this context, the following factors need attention.

Unity of the MMA

The most astonishing aspect of the success of the MMA has been its ability to bury its sectarian differences and come together under a common banner. It comprised of Maulana Shah Ahmad Noorani-led *Jamiat Ulema-e-Pakistan* (JUP) belonging to the Barelvi Sunni sect, pro-Taliban Maulana Fazl-ur-Rehman's *Jamiat Ulema-e-Islam* (JUI-F) and Sami-ul Haq's *Jamiat Ulema-e-Islam* (JUI-S) both Deobandi Sunni sects, Sajjid Mir's *Jamiat-e-Ahle Hadith*, Allama Sajjid Naqvi's *Pakistan Islami Tehrik* formerly *Tehriq-e-Jafaria* (TeJ) of the Shia sect and last and most influential, Qazi Hussain Ahmed's *Jamaat-e-Islami* (JI). Shah Ahmed Noorani[1] was the President and Qazi Hussain, the Vice-President of the party.

The coming together of Shias, Sunnis, Barelvis and Deobandis was regarded as one of the key reasons to succeed and encourage them to remain united. In an interview, Qazi Hussain Ahmed, said, "Those who came into MMA have benefited from it. Only a fool will leave it now."[2] The two schools of Sunni Islam, Deobandi and Barelvi originated from Deoband and Bareilly respectively, in the State of Uttar Pradesh in India.[3] Both were Sunni, and the major departing point in their ideology was that the Deobandi school is puritan and believes in simple ceremonies and stresses on morals and principles, whereas the Barelvi is more inclusive and follows sufism and celebrates *urs* (death anniversary). The basic theological divide between the two is over the role of the Prophet and the status of hereditary saints. The Deobandis tend to demystify the roles of saints; and the Barelvis regard saints as intermediaries to communicate with the Prophet and to seek divine salvation. The two factions of JUI are followers of the Deobandi school and followers of JUP follow the Barelvi school.[4]

The JI on the other hand, consisted of the urban, educated, professional and business elite and was considered to be more orthodox than the two schools. It is seen as more modernist than the Deobandi school. The JI also works as a bridge between different sects which are now together under the MMA. The Jamiat-e-Ahle Hadith is associated with the Wahabi sect, which follows the Prophet's tradition and not any particular school of thought as such. They seek guidance from the Saudi *Sharia* system. The lone Shia party in the MMA is the Islami Tehrik Pakistan (ITP). The Deobandis and Ahle Hadith consider Shias as infidels, who are divided into Ismailis, Bohras and Twelvers.[5]

This was not the first time when the religious parties patched up their differences for a common cause, though it was certainly the first time they allied for electoral purposes. Previously, on two occasions, it was an issue-based alliance. The Milli Yakjehti Council (MYC) of 1995 was formed to curb sectarian conflicts in Pakistan, which eventually derailed due to the JUI (F) and JUI (S) differences. In 2000, the Muttahida Inqilabi Mahaz (IMAM) was established to protest against the Western ideological and cultural invasion.[6] Through a unified forum, the MMA constituent parties were able to concentrate votes (11 per cent) in one basket, which upset the calculations of PPPP and PML-N. They focused on certain provinces like the NWFP and Balochistan and got concentrated votes.

Military-ISI-Ulema Linkage

Given the dismal electoral performance by the Islamist parties in the past, it would be fair to argue that the MMA could not have secured over 50 seats without the support of the army and the ISI. Several analysts have attributed the success of the mullahs to the pre-poll scheming and restrictions imposed by General Musharraf, which rendered the mainstream parties orphaned and mauled. The military also encouraged the militants of *Jehadi* groups to join one or the other religious party. The party, which ultimately many joined, was JUI (F). The urdu daily, *Ausaf* (October 17) reported that the MMA has been maintaining links with the terrorist groups and at one point also urged Maulana Azam Tariq, chief of banned *Sipah-e-Sahaba*, to join the MMA.[7] He is said to be a firm supporter of Musharraf's policies and currently is a Member of the National Assembly (MNA) from Jhang. It was believed that Musharraf could also use the rise of *jehadis* as a bargaining chip with the US. Nusrat Mirza endorses this view in his column in the Urdu daily, *Nawa-e-Waqt* (October 14).[8] There are reports that where hundreds of politicians were barred from contesting the elections on one ground or the other, Musharraf had directed the provincial' administrations to withdraw the cases against religious leaders and workers who were charged with the violation of code of conduct for elections, such as using loudspeakers, holding unlawful public meetings and giving incendiary speeches.[9]

The Urdu newspapers such as *Ausaf, Urdu Point* and *Nawa-e-Waqt* featured reports and editorials on how the military-ISI-*jehadi* nexus facilitated the success of the MMA. Ali Chaudhary, in his column in *Nawa-i-Waqt* (October 16) wrote that the dissenting anti-US faction in the Pakistani Army was hand in glove with the ISI and backing the religious forces. Ali also wrote that this linkage and patronage to a large extent enables the mullahs to thrive and keep the MMA conglomeration intact.[10] The PPPP attributed the rise of the MMA to military and ISI support and complained that parliamentary candidates were used and pitched selectively by them. Faratullah Babar, PPP spokesman said, "MMA's formation and victory in certain areas was facilitated to brandish to the West the threat of Islamic extremism and to show the United States that the only alternative to military rule is the rule of the mullahs."[11]

Lashkar-e-Jhangvi-Pakistan (LeJ), a Sunni terrorist group, played an instrumental role in the October elections by organising public meetings for the Islamic parties. Similarly, United Jihad Council (UJC) was active in rural Punjab where the voters preferred the Islamic parties. In the wake of 9/11 and attack on Afghanistan, Musharraf did resort to a cosmetic crackdown, but not with a long-term objective. Under pressure from the US, he did proscribe several terrorist outfits such as SSP, LeJ, Tanzeem-e-Nifaz-e-Shariat-e-Muhammadi (TNSM), Tehrik-e-Jafaria (TeJ), Lashkar-e-Toiba (LeT), and Jaish-e-Mohammad (JeM). Later, their names were changed, and their leaders were released, who then entered active politics. In the month of November 2002, Hafeez Mohammad Saeed, former chief of LeT was released, which was followed by the release of Masood Azhar, in December.[12] There was also active coordination and cooperation between the military and *jehadis* during the April Referendum. Sundeep Waslekar says, "Maximum turn out during Referendum was reported from Rawalpindi, being military headquarters, and Jhang, where most of the terrorist groups are based".[13] What makes this relationship perhaps more enduring is that the MMA, like previous Islamist parties, also needs military's support, to compensate for the lack of mass support. Late Jyotindra Nath Dixit, former Indian Foreign Secretary and Ambassador to Pakistan commented in an interview, "MMA does not have the clout to dominate the political scene, hence they need the support of the military".[14]

Marginalisation of PPPP and PML-N

In the context of incessant jostling for power between the civilians and the military in the political spectrum, General Musharraf's deliberate attempt to sideline and discriminate against the two main parties, the PPPP and the PML-N was very much expected. General Musharraf also believed, no matter how favourable the conditions, there are very slender chances of the ulema securing an absolute majority in the National Assembly. Therefore, the only viable challenge rested in its arch-rivals, the PPPP and the PML-N. He is also aware that despite having a bad experience of the democratic regimes, under Nawaz and Benazir, the public still would prefer a democratic government, provided that the new leadership shows more resolve and character. Therefore, it was natural for him to favour the Islamist parties and marginalize the non-Islamist parties. Historically too, the military has enjoyed a better relationship and understanding with the Islamist parties, than with the non-Islamist parties.

General Musharraf also made selective use of the graduation clause against the tribal candidates of the mainstream parties in the NWFP and Balochistan, whereas the Islamist parties were allowed to field their candidates having madarassa graduate degrees. Also, by implicating Benazir and Nawaz in corruption cases, and exiling them out of Pakistan, Musharraf rendered their parties disoriented. In the absence of top leadership, their parties became directionless and the second-rung leadership lacked the charisma to lift the spirits of the two parties.

9/11 and the Anti-US Sentiments

After 9/11 and the subsequent US attack on Afghanistan, anti-Americanism in Pakistan has increased dramatically. The MMA has been very vocal in its opposition to the US war in Afghanistan; its increasing interference in Pakistan's domestic affairs; an 'anti-Islam' posture; and the partisan stand on the Israel-Palestine conflict. The MMA exploited the sentiments of the public using widespread anti-Americanism to its advantage. Analyst Brigadier Shaukat Qadir said that the American actions in Afghanistan gave rise to anti-American feelings in the region. He wrote that the MMA's victory in the October elections was an indication of the growing anti-U.S. sentiments. He observed, "This is going to increase and I gravely apprehend [sic] that if the Americans keep acting unilaterally against Muslims that they are threatening to do in Iraq and Iran, then there may be a greater upsurge of this feeling of being differentiated against. You cannot have Israel doing what it is doing and expect the rest of the Muslim world to suffer under the American war against terrorism."[15]

Drive Against *Madaris*

There was a wave of anti-US sentiment sweeping across Pakistan in the wake of the crackdown waged by General Musharraf on the *jehadis* and *madaris* after 9/11 attacks. This move by General Musharraf under pressure from the US convinced the Islamist parties of the need to forge a common front to oppose Pakistan's pro-US leanings. Since 1979 the *madaris* have been the training and grooming grounds of jehadis of all shades, and this prompted General Musharraf to take action against them. He proposed a range of recommendations pertaining to *madaris'* curriculum, fund-raising, *mudarris, (pupil)* recruitment, etc., but with little success. On the issue, it should be mentioned that General Musharraf faced a twin-dilemma. First, the *madaris* play a very useful role in supplementing the State's responsibility of providing education to the poor in the far-flung areas of Pakistan and therefore purging them would be socially detrimental. And second, these *madaris* still provide a bulk of the jehadis in Jammu and Kashmir, Afghanistan and terrorist operations in other countries as well. This explains why many considered the crackdown against the *madaris* as a mere cosmetic exercise. Nevertheless, General Musharraf could show some action on curbing religious extremism purely to soothe US concerns. To pacify his domestic critics, too, he ordered the release of most detainees and made good use of them in the controversial April 2002 Referendum which was meant to legitimize his regime. In addition to the ways and means adopted by General Musharraf, the Ulema on their part urged Islamists in Pakistan to come together as a single political entity to exploit the emerging political situation in Pakistan following the US attack on Afghanistan, causing the death of a large number of Pushtuns and ouster of the Taliban regime.

MMA's Political Sagacity and Unity

Perhaps the most astonishing aspect of the success of the MMA has been its cohesiveness. It includes Maulana Shah Ahmad Noorani led *Jamiat Ulema-e-Pakistan* (JUP) belonging to the Barelvi Sunni sect, pro-Taliban Maulana Fazl-ur-Rehman's *Jamiat Ulema-e-Islam* (JUI-F) and Sami-ul Haq's *Jamiat Ulema-e-Islam* (JUI-S) both Deobandi Sunni sects, Sajjid Mir's *Jamiat-e-Ahle Hadith* (JAH), Allama Sajjid Naqvi's *Islami Tehrik Pakistan* (ITP) formerly *Tehriq-e-Jafaria* (TeJ) of the Shia sect and last and most influential Qazi Hussain Ahmed's *Jamaat-e-Islami* (JI). Noorani is the leader and Qazi Hussain, deputy leader of the MMA.

The coming together of Shias, Sunnis, Barlevis and Deobandis has surprised many. After tasting electoral success for their unity, they now look to strengthen it further, by keeping the alliance together. In an interview, Qazi Hussain Ahmed, said, "Those who came into MMA have benefited from it. Only a fool will leave it now."[16] The positive aspect of the MMA's unity is that they have risen above sectarianism and are in agreement with each other on almost all issues. The two schools of thought, Deobandi and Barelvi originated from Deoband and Bareilly respectively, in the State of Uttar Pradesh in India.[17] Both are Sunni, but the difference between the two schools is that the former is puritan and believes in simple ceremonies and stresses on morals and principles, whereas the latter is more inclusive and follows sufism and celebrates *urs* (death anniversary), unlike the Deobandis. The basic theological divide between the two is over the role of the Prophet and the status of hereditary saints. The Deobandis tend to demystify the roles of saints; and the Barelvis regard saints as intermediaries to communicate with the Prophet and to seek divine salvation. The two factions of JUI are followers of Deobandi school of thought and followers of JUP belong to the Barelvi school.[18]

The JI, which consists of the urban, educated, professional and business elite is considered to be more orthodox than the two schools but more modernist than the Deobandi school. The JI works as a bridge between different sects which are now together under the MMA. The Jamiat-e-Ahle Hadith is associated with the Wahabi sect, which follows the Prophet's tradition and not any particular school of thought as such. They seek guidance from the Saudi Sharia system. The lone Shia party in the MMA is the ITP. The Deobandis and Ahle Hadith consider Shias as infidel, who are divided into Ismailis, Bohras and Twelvers.[19]

Although this was not the first time for the Islamist parties to have patched up their differences and formed a common front, yet it was the first time when they had allied for electoral purposes. In the past on a couple of occasions, it was an issue-based alliance. The Milli Yakjehti Council (MYC) of 1995 was formed to curb sectarian conflicts in Pakistan, which eventually derailed due to the JUI (F) and JUI (S) differences. In the year 2000, 23 political and religious groups had come together in Peshawar, known as the Islami Muttahida Inqilabi Mahaz to pressurize the government to check western ideological and cultural invasion of Pakistan. But this grouping was clearly not formed for political or electoral purposes which puts it and the MYC into a different category than the MMA.

Committed Cadres and Network

MMA's election strategy could not have succeeded but for the strong cadre network. In the 2002 elections, *madaris* and cadres of various sectarian groups operated full throttle in organizing meetings, campaigning and providing stiff competition to its opponents in the field. According to a survey there are 6,000 *madaris* in Pakistan. 2,333 belong to the Deobandi school of thought; 1,625 to the Barelvi sect; 224 to the Ahle Hadith; and 163 to the Shia sect. In addition, 815 are affiliated with Jamiat-ul-Islam (F); 58 with Jamiat-ul-Islam (S); 120 with Jamiat-ul-Pakistan; 67 with Sipah-e-Sahaba, 119 with

Tehrik-e-Jafria; and 2,969 are miscellaneous.[20] These highly disciplined, trained and motivated political forces were behind the success of the MMA. Khurram Dastgir Khan says, "These *madaris* have filled a need created by rising unemployment and the collapse of state education. There is no entry test, no fees, and the room and board is free. For an unemployed, indigent teenager willing to undergo the rigmarole, enrolment in a *madaris* provides an ascriptive dignity, prospect of employment in new mosques and in the burgeoning mehfil/dars industry, in addition to spiritual rewards and salvation."[21] These *madaris* volunteered people for organizing meetings, rallies, mobilizing votes, and also guarding polling booths. The cadres of the PPPP, PML-N and other political opponents were no match for these committed party workers.

Ideological Bankruptcy of Disjointed Mainstream Parties

Over the years, the disenchantment in the public, especially with the PPPP and PML-N increased manifold, because of widespread corruption, embezzlements, nepotism, and mis-governance. In addition to their poor performance between 1998-1999, in the 2002 elections they failed to take a stand on Musharraf's controversial Referendum, US' attack on Afghanistan, Legal Framework Order (LFO), restoration of democracy and one-man-one-post. Such lack of character undermined their credentials and strengthened the *locus standi* of the mullahs. Rasul Baksh Rais, says, "Never have the people of Pakistan voted in such large numbers for the Islamist parties before...Again this change is not confined to the old, ignorant, rural peoples, but the young, urban and professional class seems to be tilting toward the Islamist parties...But the trend is visible and if the mainstream political parties continue to ignore the fundamental issues of good governance, good state and society, the general public including the middle class may embrace the fold of Islamist parties."[22]

The MMA, on the other hand, has been very vocal against America's high-handed tactics in Afghanistan and its interference in Pakistan's domestic and foreign policies. They also continued to maintain pressure on Musharraf on the above issues and condemned the US bombing of Iraq in which several innocent civilians were killed. Compared to the issue-driven campaign of the MMA, the conduct of the non-Islamist parties has been vacuous and spineless.

MMA's Provincial Strategy

As opposed to Maulana Qazi Hamidullah who said that the mission of Mutahidda Majlis-i-Amal Pakistan (MMAP) is not to rule but to enforce the *Sharia* laws in the country,[23] the MMA donned a rather liberal face before the elections. They called for equal rights for the minorities; expressed willingness to settle the Kashmir issue through peaceful dialogue under the Simla Accord and maintain a cordial and non-confrontationist relationship with the West, especially the US. The MMA's Secretary General and the party's prime ministerial candidate, Maulana Fazl-ur Rehman said, "Pakistan and its people have a clear policy on Kashmir as they want its solution according to the UN resolutions and under the spirit of the Simla Agreement."[24] The MMA was aware of the popular perception of the public of their political agenda and it was important not to highlight their hidden agenda during the elections. Their election manifesto, too, was prepared with care by avoiding controversial issues such as the implementation of *Sharia*, educational segregation, status of women, etc.[25] They also chose not to attack Musharraf too much, at such an early stage, when the military was playing a dominant role in masterminding the elections. The MMA's accommodative approach pleased Musharraf and he showed a noticeable bias towards them. As mentioned earlier, the military and ISI had a tacit understanding with the religious groups who were actively engaged in the April Referendum. Since April 2002, Musharraf and the Islamist parties had realized how important it was for both to have an understanding. This created a situation in which the MMA and its *madaris* were exempted from several curbs, which were imposed on the other parties. For instance, none of the non-Islamist parties were allowed to hold any public rally in Rawalpindi, whereas MMA and its constituent parties were exempted from such a prohibition.

Balochistan

Nationalist parties like the Awami National Party always used to be the driving political force in Balochistan which ceased to be the case in 2002. The King's party or the PML-Q topped the results tally followed by the MMA which became the former's coalition partner in the province. The MMA's success in Balochistan can be attributed to two factors. First, after the withdrawal of the Soviet Union from Afghanistan and its subsequent breakup, there was an ideological vacuum, which the Baloch nationalists failed to fill. This ideological bankruptcy split the Baloch nationalists and there was no single platform to assemble and execute their political objectives. Second, the Baloch or the secular nationalists also failed to take any stand whatsoever on the US attack on Afghanistan. As a result, they ended up appearing pro-Musharraf on several issues, especially the US attack on Afghanistan, which was exploited by the MMA in the elections.[26] The MMA's anti-US rhetoric paid rich dividends in Balochistan and they were also successful in projecting themselves as being against Musharraf's US policies. The MMA's issue-based political strategy benefited it and they also managed to outsmart the Baloch nationalists through their ideological and electoral rhetoric.

NFWP

In NWFP the ethnic factor (Pukhtun) rather than religious was more dominant which was exploited by the MMA. The party won most of the seats in Pukhtun-dominated areas and lost out in the non-Pukhtun areas of Abbotabad, Haripur and Manshera in NWFP. Likewise, in the Pukhtun areas of Balochistan like Zhob, Pishin, and Loralai, the MMA achieved better results. In Baloch-dominated areas Baloch nationalists along with PML-Q, made their presence felt.[27]

The sympathy wave for the MMA came due to the US attack on Afghanistan which killed a large number of Pukhtuns in Afghanistan. The US drive against Pukhtuns in Afghanistan happened to be the key issue drawing vehement criticism by the Pukhtun elements in JUI (F) and JI, within the MMA. They organized massive rallies opposing US strikes against Pukhtuns, who in return considered the MMA as the champions of the cause of the Afghan Pukhtuns.

Pukhtun sympathy for the MMA also developed as Pukhtun nationalist were seen more as anti-Taliban and pro-American, which is why even PPP (Aftab Sherpao) won more seats than the Awami National Party (ANP) for showing more concern and solidarity with the Afghan Pukhtuns.

Sindh

The MMA adopted a different election strategy in Sindh where it won five out of 20 NA seats and only losing the remaining 15 in a stiff fight. Its successes in Karachi and Hyderabad came about for primarily two reasons. First, the MMA managed to exploit the sentiments of the people against the US' war on Afghanistan and excessive interference in Pakistan's internal matters. Second, it successfully utilized the anti-incumbency factor against the MQM.[28]

The MMA focused its entire election campaign highlighting local issues such as health, education, civic concerns and most importantly the *Bhatta* (extortion) which impressed thousands of shopkeepers and businessmen. The MQM leadership, which was seen as more pro-Musharraf, was severely hit by the people's apathy towards them. There were reports about their ill-planned political campaigns and lack of mobilization of voters. A large number of their traditional voters claimed that they did not vote for them because the MQM party workers did not mobilize them. Also, the entire MQM political campaign was locked in an inter-factional (Altaf and Haqiqui) feud.[29] On the one hand, the MMA managed to expose the failure of MQM in delivering the goods to the public, on the other, it not only used its strong cadre for mobilizing people on the polling day, but also in organizing rallies and meetings for the MMA leaders.

Peoples' Antipathy to General Musharraf's April Referendum

During the 2002 elections there was a substantial resentment over the April 30 Referendum, which Musharraf held to sustain himself for another five-year term. Before going into the general elections, Musharraf wanted to consolidate his position and authority and guard against any political ouster, which victorious anti-military political parties could have engineered. Like Zia-ul Haq, General Musharraf very cleverly framed the question to be asked to the people which mixed his election with several pressing issues which the country faced. In other words, he calculated that even if people disapproved of him as an efficient leader and deemed him unfit to be a President, they would nevertheless vote for him on the basis of issues. The question put in the Referendum for voting for General Musharraf said, "For the survival of the local government system, establishment of democracy, continuity of reforms, end to sectarianism and extremism, and to fulfill the vision of Quaid-e-Azam, would you like to elect President General Musharraf as President of Pakistan for five years?"[30] The Referendum was questioned on constitutional grounds and revealed that Musharraf was unwilling to relinquish his position and sought to legitimize military's re-entry into active mainstream politics. Several petitions, including Qazi Hussain Ahmed's, questioned the legality of the Referendum, but nothing substantial could be ruled against the Referendum.[31] Criticisms were levelled from all parties calling it unconstitutional since there was no provision in the Constitution for holding Referendum for the office of President.[32] The Human Rights Commission of Pakistan also questioned it, calling the voters as 'captive voters'.[33] Musharraf's credibility suffered a severe dent, which was exploited by the MMA and the ire of the people against him was reflected in the October 2002 elections. However, in June 2003, in a major setback to the opposition of Musharraf's election through a Referendum, the Lahore High Court, rejecting a petition filed by the Lawyer's Forum, validated the Referendum, saying that it did not impinge upon any constitutional provision.[34]

Conclusion

The rise of the Islamist parties was enabled by both internal and external factors. At the domestic level, support of the military establishment which also marginalized the moderate parties had put the MMA's constituent parties in an advantageous position. In addition, the wave of anti-Americanism in the wake of war in Afghanistan and crackdown on the extremists in Pakistan became the catalyst for MMA's political unity and electoral success. The victory of the MMA with over 60 seats in the National Assembly and its coming to power in two provinces was undoubtedly going to create problems for democracy and General Musharraf's military regime sooner or later. It was a matter of time before the tiger that General Musharraf rode for over four years began to show its teeth to the master. Blinded by the short-term gains of his alliance with the Islamists, General Musharraf made a serious mistake of ignoring the long-term losses for himself and Pakistan. He used the Islamist parties and groups to consolidate himself constitutionally and marginalize the moderate parties and create a resistance-free political set-up. His preoccupation with the political stability at the Centre allowed the MMA to unleash a vigorous Islamization drive in the NWFP with adverse consequence for the entire country.

In Pakistan's history, Islamists have learnt to implement their agenda either through force or through cooperation with the military regimes as seen in their engagement with different regimes in the 1950s, the 70s and the 80s. Military regimes have shown a visible bias towards the Islamist parties due to their aversion for democracy and moderate parties and the unanimity over intrusive and hegemonic nature of the State. The 'Islam card' has perennially remained the primary tool for gaining legitimacy and public support and no different was the case with General Musharraf. The military had come to power in Pakistan after eleven years and it was gearing itself to stay in power for a long time, and to achieve this, no price was too costly to pay for General Musharraf. He made no qualms about undermining democracy and promoting the Islamists as the alternative. His support to the MMA it seems emanated from a false sense of confidence that he would have little difficulty in containing the Islamists when the situation demanded, unlike in the case of moderate parties, such as the PPPP and PML-N. It was a marriage of convenience in which both parties had readily agreed to share power without rocking the boat. As the old adage goes—power corrupts and absolute power corrupts absolutely, their alliance was inherently very complicated and cracks began to emerge as soon as both sides began to act in the manner which did not conform to their original understanding of power-sharing. The following chapter examines the implications of MMA's political ideology and policies on democracy and the dangers that their Islamization drive poses to peace and stability in Pakistan. The chapter also illuminates the complexities and contradictions of the military-MMA alliance and the dangers of General Pervez Musharraf's alliance with the Islamist parties.

NOTES

1. Maulana Shah Ahmed Noorani died in December 2003 and was succeeded by Qazi Hussain Ahmed as the MMA President. Shah Fareed-ul Haq became the JUP leader after Anas Noorani, son of Maulana Noorani refused to take over. See Amir Wasim, "Maulana Noorani Passes Away", at http://www.dawn.com/2003/12/12/top2.htm
2. M. Ilyas Khan, Interview with Qazi Hussain Ahmed, *The Herald*. November 2002. p. 56.
3. For detailed information on Islamic groups and movements please see Talmiz Ahmad—*An Introduction to Contemporary Islamic Groups and Movements in India,* Author's Publications, 2001.
4. ICG Asia Report No. 49. pp. 5-6.
5. Ibid.
6. Ibid.
7. Strategic Foresight Group, "Window on Pakistan: Rise of Hardliners", The *Times of India,* New Delhi, October 21, 2002.
8. Ibid.
9. Shamim-ur-Rehman, "Did Govt. Strike Deal with MMA?" at http://www.dawn.com/2002/12/30/top6.htm.
10. Ibid.
11. ICG Asia Report No. 49. March 20, 2003. p. 15.
12. For details see "Pakistan's Militant Islamic Groups", at http://

news.bbc.co.uk/1/hi/world/south_asia/1758534.stm. Also see, 'Pak Court Sets Free Jaish Chief Azhar'. The *Sunday Times of India*, December 15, 2002.

13. Speaking at Hotel Oberoi, New Delhi on "*Future of Pakistan*", October 30, 2002.
14. Interview with the Author. February 10, 2003.
15. Shaukat Qadir, "Pakistani Islamists Stage Anti-US Demonstration", January 3, 2003 at http://www.naviquest.com/812313459.htm.
16. M. Ilyas Khan, Interview with Qazi Hussain Ahmed, *The Herald*. November 2002. p. 56.
17. For detailed information on Islamic groups and movements see Talmiz Ahmad, *An Introduction to Contemporary Islamic Groups and Movements in India no 3.* Author's Publications, 2001.
18. ICG Asia Report no. 4.
19. Ibid.
20. Mutahir Ahmed, "MMA's victory: Implications for Pakistan", at http://www.jang.com.pk/thenews/oct2002-weekly/nos-20-10-2002/pol1.htm
21. Khurram Dastgir Khan, "The Coming Theocracy" at http://www.jang.com.pk/thenews/nov2002-daily/02-11-2002/oped/o2.htm.
22. Rasul Baksh Rais, "Rise of Islamist parties", *The News,* October 19, 2002 at www.jang.com.pk/thenews/oct2002-daily/ 19-10-2002/oped/opinion.htm
23. "MMA to Enforce Shariat Laws" at www.dawn.com/2002/10/17/nat8.htm.
24. "MMA to Fulfill Pledges Made to World: Leaders Assure Diplomats" at http://www.dawn/2002/10/24/top 2.htm.
25. See Appendix II.
26. Mutahir Ahmed, no. 21.
27. Reza Rehman Khan Qazi, The Political Economy of MMA's Victory, at http://www.jang.com.pk/thenews/oct2002-weekly/nos-20-10-2002/pol1.htm#6
28. Hussain Askari, "Another Muttahida", *The Herald,* November 2002, p. 48.
29. Ibid.
30. Pervez Musharraf, *In the Line of Fire: A Memoir*, Simon and Shuster, London, 2006, p. 167.

31. B. Murlidhar Reddy, "Musharraf's Case Hearing on April 22", *The Hindu*. April 17, 2002.
32. "PML Launches Drive Against Referendum" at http://www.dawn.com/2002/04/13/nat3.htm.
33. ICG Asia Report, No. 10, p. 20.
34. K.J.M. Varma, "Musharraf can Continue as Army Chief rules HC", The *Economic Times*, June 12, 2003.

CHAPTER III

MMA and Islamisation

Extreme Measures

It was a matter of time to find the Muttahida Majlis-e-Amal (MMA) after having achieved unprecedented success, starting to push its Islamisation agenda, begining with the North West Frontier Province. It was an eventuality that General Pervez Musharraf himself must have long anticipated, though he was not fully cognizant of its actual content and scope. This chapter focuses on a wide range of Islamisation measures that the MMA introduced in the NWFP and sought to export to other provinces as well. The NWFP, as the subsequent analysis would show, had become the Islamisation laboratory of the MMA, particularly the Jamaat-e-Ulema Islam (F) party, which was heading the majority government there. This chapter also captures the complications that Islamisation caused in the Military-MMA alliance, causing a great deal of discomfort for General Musharraf and his regime.

Before the elections the Islamist parties were well aware of their limitations and weak political base in Pakistan. Their dismal record in past elections always loomed large on the psyche of their leaders and cadres and kept them alert in order to exploit any opportunity that may help them overcome their weaknesses. The previous chapter explained how the MMA forged an alliance with the Military which not only strengthened their political muscle but also enabled them to escape various electoral laws such as those pertaining to the graduate clause and criminal record. Their madrassa degrees were recognised as legitimate graduate degrees and many MMA leaders saw cases against them dropped to qualify for elections. Assured of such favours from the establishment, the party now needed to move beyond its traditional vote bank and impress upon the liberal and moderate-minded population. It was wise on the MMA's part to have toned down its radical and anti-democracy image by charting a moderate manifesto. The 15-point election manifesto released in the 2002 elections said that the MMA would 'make Pakistan a true Islamic welfare state to ensure justice to people and eradicate corruption whatsoever'... 'create an independent, just and humane economic system where citizens will be provided opportunities for *halal* jobs, business and investments'... (and) 'protect rights of women guaranteed by Islam and restoration of their honour and prestige[1]. The manifesto, it must be emphasized, on many counts, gave a moderate impression and its language was perhaps deliberately kept soft to ward off negative public reactions. Incidentally, the party was accorded 'book' as the election symbol and the leaders used every occasion to flaunt it as the 'Holy Quran' during the election rallies and campaigns.[2] The slogans were coined likewise. For instance, '*Mulk Bachao, Kitab Par Muhar Lagao*' (save the nation, vote for book), *Hathon Mei Kitab Ho, Agaz-e-Inqalab Ho*' (with the book in hand, let the revolution begin), '*Ek Millat, Ek Parcham, Ek Mission, Kitab Hamara Mustakbil*' (one community, one flag, one symbol, book our future) were coined to present the election symbol as more than just a book.[3]

Gloves Off Post-Election

The MMA government under Akram Khan Durrani in the NWFP pushed its Islamisation agenda vigorously which included many measures which had not found mention in its election manifesto for obvious reasons. After taking charge in the province the JUI-F leadership seemed convinced that in the long-term interest of the party it was essential to adhere to its fundamental principles and policies and push the Islamisation drive. They also seemed confident that they would be confronting little opposition from the Centre and General Pervez Musharraf for the support they were rendering to the latter in the National Assembly. This also explains that why

General Musharraf and his PML-Q regime largely ignored the Islamisation drive underway in the NWFP until it began to transform into a national drive and endanger General Musharraf's own enlightened moderation policies. Some of the key Islamisation measures undertaken by the MMA are as follows.

Enforcement of *Sharia*

On June 2, 2003, as per some Urdu dailies' reports the NWFP Assembly passed the controversial *Sharia* bill which called for a ban on bank interest (*riba*) and reverting to Fridays as a holiday. The bill also provided for the implementation of the recommendation of the Council for Islamic Ideology (CII) in the province. The CII recommended that no tax should be levied on weapons, houses and vehicles. The bill also called for segregation in education (separate seating for women) and making *Hijab* (scarf) compulsory for women; ultrasound of women to be done by female doctors; prohibition on male coaches training women athletes; closing down cinemas and cable networks; and replacement of trousers and shirts with *salwar and kameez* as school uniform. Another report mentioned that though the PML-Q and PML-N members opposed making Friday a holiday, they agreed for the removal of *riba* (interest) from bank transactions.[4] The *Jang* reported the creation of a committee by the NWFP government which recommended the enforcement of Islamic punishment such as stoning to death, amputation of limbs and death penalty for blasphemy and consumption of liquor.[5] There were also reports of banning the Basant celebrations. Qazi Hussain Ahmed and PML-Q parliamentarian Samina Naveed urged the government to frame laws at the earliest for banning Basant celebrations.[6]

Hisbah Bill

MMA's own version of NSC, the 14-member, *Nifaz-e-Shariat Council* constituted by Akram Khan Durrani, monitors implementation of Islamic rules and reforms in the government departments. In a major move, the NWFP Assembly passed the Hisbah Bill of 14 July 2005 which provides for the creation of a Taliban-like 'Ministry for

Promotion of Virtue and Prevention of Vice'.[7] The bill provided for a *mohtasib* of the 'ministry' who would be unaccountable to anyone and all courts would be barred from reviewing its decision or granting stays against its orders. In other words, under the Hisbah Bill, no right of appeal would be possible.[8]

The opposition labeled it as a "parallel judicial system", and "martial law of the mullahs".[9] It must be noted that according to Articles 145-152 of the Constitution, the National Assembly has the overriding authority of reversing legislation of any provincial assembly.[10] General Musharraf himself had expressed serious reservation against the legislation of the bill.[11] The joy of the *Ulema* proved shortlived with the Supreme Court in August 2005 ruling several clauses in the bill to be contrary to the Constitution. The apex court advised the NWFP Assembly to present an amended bill for legislative perusal. The Supreme Court blocked the bill saying that it (Hisbah Bill) would have further undermined the already fragile democratic ethos in Pakistan and pushed the country towards rapid Islamisation.[12] The MMA pushed hard to run the NWFP along the Taliban model. Envisioning the Taliban-like governance, Maulana Fazl-ur Rehman submitted, "We want to create an atmosphere where every Muslim abides by Islamic laws, enabling us to establish a true Islamic welfare state first in the Frontier and then gradually in the whole country...The Taliban...was an ideal Islamic system, but they were trying to implement it by force. But here in Pakistan, we are trying to bring about an Islamic revolution in accordance with the wishes of the people who voted for us."[13] The MMA accorded top priority to the Hisbah Bill and it remained so despite the Supreme Court stay against it which is why a year later the NWFP Assembly presented a revised bill and passed a watered down version. The interesting aspect of the passing of the bill this time was that some opposition legislators, including the liberals as well reportedly voted for the bill against the advise of their parliamentary leaders. The bill provided for an anti-vice ombudsman enjoying sweeping powers to implement *Sharia* and forbid persons, agencies and authorities working under the administrative control of the government to act against *Sharia.*[14] However, the bill was vehemently opposed by Awami National Party (ANP), PPP (Sherpao), and PPPP. Interestingly, PML voted against the bill but one of its legislators voted in favour. The leader of the opposition in the Assembly, Shahzada Gistasip questioned the purpose and legality of the bill arguing that it was repugnant to the existing laws and provisions in view of the Supreme Court. As per the Article 116 of the 1973 Constitution, the Bill also required the signature of the Governor Ali Mohammad Jan Aurakzai, as previously, his predecessor, Iftikhar Hussain Shah had refused to sign the bill.[15] The biggest challenge before the party was securing the Federal approval for the bill. The Supreme Court had been requested by the petitioner, Maulvi Iqbal Haider, Chairman Awami Himayat Tehrik, to declare the bill unconstitutional and repugnant to the apex court's 2005 recommendations. The petition claimed that the bill would create serious constitutional issues entailing administrative anarchy among the federating units of the country and create a parallel system of law and order. The petition also said that in the absence of appropriate changes in Sections 12, 23, 27, 25 (1 and 2) and section 28 of the original bill would violate Articles 2 A (Objective Resolution), 4 (rights of individuals to be dealt with in accordance with the law), 9 (security of person), 14 (inviolability of dignity of man), 16 (freedom of assembly), 17 (freedom of association), 18 (freedom of trade, business or profession), 19 (freedom of speech), 20 (freedom to profess religion and manage religious institutions), 25 (equality of citizens) and 175 (establishment and jurisdiction of courts). The petition also mentioned that on September 6, 2004 even the CII had cautioned the provincial government against the possibility of the bill being exploited for political purposes.[16]

In 2005, apart from the *Sharia* and Hisbah bills the MMA legislators tabled two more bills namely, the 'NWFP Prohibition of Dancing and Music Bill, 2005' and the 'NWFP Prohibition of Use of Women in Photograph Bill, 2005'. After the bill is passed, music and dance in public places and educational institutions, and using photographs of women in advertisements be declared penal offences punishable by up to five years in jail plus a fine of Rs. 5,000 to 10,000.[17] The MMA has already imposed ban on music in public transport and the MMA activists have warned the musicians in Peshawar to shut down their business, calling it 'evil and un-Islamic'[18]

The MMA activists smashed billboards featuring women in advertisements. In another incident, a group of MMA activists attacked a circus in Gujranwala in Punjab, setting the tent on fire, injuring over 100 people. Rakshanda Naz of the Aurat Foundation, an NGO in Peshawar, says that the people cannot afford to show any dissent because of the death threats from the Islamists.[19]

There have been other issues in addition to the Hisbah Bill. The government and the MMA had voted together in the National Assembly to kill a PML-Q member's bill seeking to put curbs on honour killings or *Karo Kari*. The Code of Criminal Procedure (Amendment) Bill had sought to amend the existing law to make *Karo Kari* a non-compoundable offence. The PPPP debated that the State should be given the status of 'wali' who can grant the pardon, and not the father or brothers of a killer, to prevent families from conspiring with outsiders to commit the killing. The MMA argued that any interference by the State cannot be accepted in religion and joined the government in defeating the bill.[20]

Legal System

Framing the Pakistani legal system in accordance with the Sharia laws was not a new development under the MMA. In 1979, during General Zia's rule four ordinances, also known as the Hudood ordinances, were issued which prescribed punishment according to Islamic law; such as death penalties, flogging, amputation of limbs, stoning for theft, adultery, blasphemy etc.[21] In addition to the Supreme Court and high courts-General Zia also established the Federal Sharia Court (FSC), to supercede the jurisdiction of the Supreme Court and high courts on matters pertaining to implementation of Islamic laws. The FSC, which established a parallel judicial system, in May 1980, was a serious blow to the supremacy of Parliament. Article 230-D of the Constitution empowers the court to strike down any statute law, which may be deemed repugnant to the injunctions of Islam.[22] In 1991, Enforcement of Sharia Act was passed which made *Sharia* the supreme law of the land. The Act said, 'The *Sharia* that is to say the Injunctions of Islam as laid in the Holy Qur'an and Sunnah, shall be the supreme law of Pakistan.'[23]

The Islamisation of the legal system was revived by the MMA in the NWFP, and in the National Assembly it maintained a constant pressure on General Musharraf and the PML-Q government to support the implementation of *Sharia* at the national level. It urged the Government to strengthen the FSC through the constitutional amendments and by inducting more *Ulema* to run the FSC. The MMA also demanded reversion to the 1973 Constitution to restore the Islamic identity of Pakistan. Shah Ahmed Noorani said, "Pakistan came into being in the name of Islam. Its Constitution is also Islamic. Therefore its Islamic identity and 1973 Constitution should be restored."[24] It would be fair to mention that although the MMA has an advantage in the NWFP, as far as implementation of the *Sharia* laws are concerned, but it is also aware at the same time that its Islamisation agenda would not have widespread support outside the province. To implement its Islamic agenda outside the NWFP the MMA has to take the support of the federal government which has been lacking on major issues such as the Hisbah Bill. On less significant issues the government from time to time has tried to accommodate the MMA's concerns so as to keep them under some federal obligations.

Status of Women

In Pakistan, women have been subject to discrimination in various forms, and the MMA's political agenda, which, although claimed to uplift the status of women, in practice eroded their socio-economic rights. The party has followed an inconsistent policy on the issue of women. In Pakistan women were granted the right of franchise under the 1956 Constitution, which was soon abrogated in 1958. The 1973 Constitution provided 20 reserved seats for women under Article 51(4). In the 2002 elections, reserved seats for women included 60 for the National Assembly, 17 for the Senate, 66 for provincial assemblies in Punjab, 29 in Sindh, 22 in NWFP and 11 in Balochistan.[25] In principle, the MMA had been against women's participation in political and public life and hence it was quite encouraging to see more women candidates in the National Assembly. It appears that the MMA chose power over ideology and as a result 12 MMA women candidates were elected to the National Assembly, including Qazi Hussain Ahmed's daughter and Maulana Fazl-ur Rehman's three sisters-in-law. The party had also put many women candidates in the fray for provincial assemblies. Hafiz Hashmat, MMA's Minister for Women, Development said, "We want women to have the status given to them by Islam as mothers, wives and sisters, but we will not force them to follow the Islamic code of behaviour. We will not use force but persuasion and education."[26] This statement can be interpreted as outlining women's key responsibilities only within the household as mothers, sister and wives than anything else, indicating the party's disapproval of working women. The MMA's vision for the women becomes all the more clear when one looks at the CII recommendations which MMA pushed for implementation. The recommendations provided: veil to be mandatory for women; veil-observing women should not be forced to submit photos for employment; women should not be asked to receive foreigners at airports; men's entry should be banned in female hospitals, especially gynaecology wards; women should not go to male doctors, nor get clothes stitched from male tailors; and family planning policy should be withdrawn as it is un-Islamic and increasing population is not a burden on the economy.[27] In contrast, the JI had a totally different role to offer to the women. It vowed to provide women basic military training and make the controversial Hudood Ordinance consonant with the teachings of the Holy Quran. Reports suggested that women would be given rifle training and JI would urge the government to arrange funds for such training.[28]

However, notwithstanding the JI's plans, the MMA's stand on women is rather discouraging. It had no qualms with backing Islamic laws which are considered anti-women, such as Hudood and *Karo Kiri*, ironically with the support of its women legislators, the NWFP Assembly and the National Assembly.

Hudood Ordinance

In 1979, General Zia-ul-Haq had promulgated four ordinances popularly known as the Hudood Ordinance for providing protection against offences such as non-marital rape (*Zina-bil-Jabr*), extramarital sex (*zina*), gambling, alcohol, and property-related offences. The ordinance prescribed punishment according to Islamic law, such as death penalties, flogging, amputation of limbs, and stoning for theft, adultery and blasphemy.[29] In September 2003, the National Commission on the Status of Women (NCSW) had recommended amendments in the Hudood Ordinance which was rejected in the NWFP Assembly. The MMA's women legislators rejected the recommendations saying that nobody had the right to amend the laws enshrined in the Holy Qur'an. The MMA legislators also had the support of the PML-Q women legislators on the issue.[30] In the National Assembly, the women MMA legislators advised the government not to touch the Hudood Ordinance at this crucial juncture when the country was passing through a serious constitutional crisis. They warned that the consequences would be "very serious" and "there was a majority of women in Parliament who loved Islam and Pakistan irrespective of their party affiliation".[31]

In October 2003, the PPPP moved a bill in the National Assembly calling for the repeal of the Hudood Ordinance but the bill was defeated.[32] The MMA opposed the move and Qazi Hussain Ahmed categorically told the then Prime Minister Zafarullah Khan Jamali that the MMA would not support the creation of NSC if the Hudood Ordinance was repealed. As a result, the latter had assured that the no changes would be made in the Hudood Ordinance, let alone repealing it.[33]

Hudood laws have always been at the centre of intense debates between various groups and political parties. Over the years, gradually, a consensus has been emerging endorsed both by the PML-Q led-cabinet as well as General Musharraf that these laws needed to be amended if not repealed. The content and nature of the amendment was debated when the bill was again tabled in the National Assembly in August 2006.[34] The federal government and the MMA have always been at loggerheads over the issue. In 2003s the MMA had succeeded in defeating the bill moved in by the PPPP which called for the scrapping of the ordinance. The government at the Centre was initially reluctant to trigger any unwarranted controversy by raking the issue through debate in Parliament. However, as a part of the enlightened moderation which General Musharraf has been championing since 2001, he has been consciously trying to alter Pakistan's conservative and anti-progressive image especially with regard to the status of women and implementation of *Sharia*. The Mukhtar Mai and Dr. Shaizia Khalid episodes came as a bolt from the blue which again showed the lopsidedness of Islamic laws in dealing with rape victims.[35] Although the two cases turned out to be more political issues rather than social, nevertheless they necessitated concrete measures to deal with excesses against women in Pakistan. General Musharraf's Military regime was facing all-round embarrassment as the reports of government mishandling began to do rounds in the domestic and international media. The move to amend the Hudood Ordinance was also driven by the motive to undo the wrongs and mishandling of these two cases and improve the regime's tarnished image.

After several months of exchange of heated debates and dialogues between the government and the MMA constituents, coupled with political threats issued by the latter's side for withdrawing support to the government if the ordinance was repealed or amended, the government finally mustered sufficient political will to pass the Protection of Women's (Criminal Laws Amendment) Rights Bill for necessary amendments in the ordinance. The bill was passed by the 342-seat National Assembly on November 15, 2006. The MMA as expected staged a walkout amidst slogan-chanting by its members. The PPPP, despite being a vehement critic of the current government, decided to support the government on this vital issue.[36] A week later the 100-member Senate passed the bill amidst protest by the MMA who threatened to resign if the bill was passed. In a overwhelming 'yes' vote the PML-Q majority Senate with support from moderate parties, including the PPPP, passed the bill which was to become law with the signature of the President and amend the 27-year old Hudood Ordinance brought into force by General Zia-ul Haq. The PPPP parliamentary group leader Raza Rabbani clarified that his party's support was only issue-based and should not be construed as endorsement of Pervez Musharraf's policy of 'enlightened moderation'. Although PML-N abstained in the voice voting, saying that the bill should have been referred to the CII.[37] A vociferous MMA was highly enraged with the passing of the bill and warned that its members in the National Assembly would resign over the issue by December 7, 2006. Qazi Hussain Ahmed, President of the MMA, in the Supreme Council meeting said," We will submit our combined resignation in the next session in the National Assembly; I have received all the resignations."[38] However, the division within the MMA became apparent on the issue of resignation at least and this was not the first time that a crack had emerged within the conglomeration. Maulana Fazl-ur Rehman though expressed his displeasure with the passing of the bill but he said that the MMA must tread the path cautiously in a step-by-step manner instead of any undue haste. In the past there had been division within the MMA, especially between Fazl-ur Rehman's JUI-F and JI on the question of attending the NSC meeting with the JUI-F in favour of attending the meeting. The JUI-F runs a majority government in NWFP and is a coalition partner in Balochistan with the PML-Q and clearly had not wanted to complete the full term. An articulate Maulana Fazl-ur Rehman clarified that resignation was not the only way to pressurize the government and the party must look into achieving its purpose by being in the system. He echoed the sentiments of the ARD and PML-N legislators who believed that the MMA must join hands with the opposition in a country-wide protest and only resign at an opportune time.[39] Subsequently, Fazl-ur Rehman announced that JUI-F legislators would not resign from the National Assembly. The decision cast shadows over the conglomeration's unity and the final decision in the matter in principle rested with the MMA's 18-member Supreme Council.[40] The division within the MMA was fundamental in nature which was superficially buried for political purposes in the run-up to the elections. The ensuring wedge within the MMA also reflected the larger grievances with the constituent parties carried against each other. In the past the domination of the JUI-F and the JI in the MMA had caused a rift with the JUI-P which subsequently broke away from the conglomeration. To JUI-F's advantage, the federal government on its part ruled out any early polls and Chaudhary Shujaat Hussain, President of PML, announced that the Coordination

Committee would be formed to look into whether provisions in the new bill were un-Islamic. He expressed hope that the MMA leaders would not resign since the government was ready to talk to them on the issue.[41] It was apparent that the government was treading very cautiously on the issue and did not want any unnecessary complications to arise out of the confrontation.

The passage of the controversial Women's Protection Bill created scope for new political alignments along 'ideological lines' between friends and friends, foes and foes and between friends and foes as well. The PPPP's decision to vote in favour of the bill could be the catalyst for a prospective political understanding with General Musharraf and the PML-Q wherein the liberals together take on the mullahs in the next elections, although the PPPP called for a grand opposition consisting of the ARD and the MMA constituent parties against the Military-supported PML-Q regime. Having said that, there always remains enough scope for a last minute understanding with the government should Benazir Bhutto be allowed to make a comeback. PML-N on the other hand, abstained from voting and criticised the PPPP for voting in favour of the bill. The PML-N also was wise to remain within the ARD and also keep its option of a prospective alliance with the MMA open. The MMA on its part was eager to win the trust of the ARD parties and join the front against General Musharraf. The biggest problem however, was to undo its past 'dealings' with the Military regime and provide justification for its intensive Islamisation drive.

Registration of Madaris

On June 1, 2004 the federal government lifted the ban on the registration of *madaris* which was imposed in 1994. This meant that as per the Societies Act of 1860, all kinds of religious seminaries would have to register and provide the necessary information of their activities, structure and administration.[42] Earlier, General Musharraf had promulgated the Madrassa Registration and Regulation Ordinance in 2002, which lapsed three months later. In the post-September 11 period, he strongly felt the need to streamline the workings of the *madaris* in Pakistan, which was suspected of training *jehadis.* The registration drive was being carried out under the 1860 Act which authorised only the provincial governments for the registration of the *madaris,* which the federal government sought to bring under the purview of the Centre, and under a single ministry.[43] The NWFP initiated the registration process and Maulana Amanullah Haqqani, the province's Religious Affairs Minister said that the registration would go ahead but no changes would be brought about in the curriculum of the *madaris* and he expected 1,500 new *madaris* to register.[44] The registration drive though faced stiff opposition from the seminary boards of *Deobandi, Barelvi, Shiaite,* and *Ahle Hadith* faiths. The boards formed an alliance known as *Ittehad Tanzeematul Madaris al-Deeniya* (ITMD), to negotiate with the government which also accused the JUI-F and JI of ignoring the interest of the other faiths and expressed reservations against providing detailed information on the workings of the *madaris* to the government. The federal government clarified that to secure government assistance, all the seminaries have to register and provide information on sources of funding, numbers of students, origin of students and teachers, and curriculum. The MMA remained a divided house on this issue, since the Barelvi *madaris,* which supposedly were never part of the Afghan *jihad* did not want to share information because of the questionable activities of the Deobandi *madaris.*[45] Given the difficulties that the registration drive involved and the resources it required, the Centre brought it under the purview of the NSC.[46]

Passport Controversy over Religion Column

The MMA made an issue out of a non-issue and succeeded in prevailing over the government over the restoration of the religion column in the passports. Their protest was so persuasive and effective the MMA managed to get the support of even the PML-Q Chairman Chaudhary Shujaat Hussain. MMA's argument on the issue was that the deletion of the religion column would enable the non-muslims (declared so in 1974) like Qadianis to go to places of pilgrimage, which could be prevented with the religious column in the passports. Earlier, passports without the religion column were issued as per the International Civil Aviation Organization (ICAO) standards and the move was appreciated by a majority of the people. Later, buckling under pressure from the MMA, the government agreed to restore the religion column. The decision to include the religion column gave the MMA a sense of achievement and victory for its ideological contestations.[47] The National Database Registration Authority (NADRA) has begun issuing the machine-readable passports with the addition of the eighth column (religion) from March 28, 2005.[48]

Islamic Banking and Interest-Free Economy

On the economic front, the MMA's election manifesto envisaged 'to create an independent, just and humane economic system where citizens will be provided opportunities for halal jobs, business and investments'.[49] Through 'halal jobs' the party pushed for an interest-free economy wherein *riba* (interest) was abolished from all business transactions. The *riba* free transaction was an old practice, which Zia-ul Haq had introduced which imposed the pre-quranic medieval forms of *mudaraba* (profit sharing), *muzaraa* (share-cropping), *zakat* (charity), *ushr* (tithe), and *riba* (usury). Islamic or interest-free banking is being developed on the basis of the medieval concept of *mudaraba.*[50] The NWFP government was the first to introduce Islamic banking in the province when the then Prime Minister Zafarullah Khan Jamali, inaugurated the Bank of Khyber (BoK) in November 2003, approved by the State Bank of Pakistan (SBP). The MMA's plan was to convert the BoK into an Islamic banking system which was being watched with keenness by the commercial banks who were interested in knowing whether it would be a beneficial system to adopt. The fundamental principle was to abolish *riba* and base all bank transactions on profit and loss sharing.[51] In November 1991, the federal *Sharia* Court (FSC) had declared, that all interest-based financial transactions would be considered un-Islamic and illegal. Although, neither the Benazir Bhutto nor Nawaz Sharif governments implemented the order, yet on December 23, 1999, the Sharia Appellate bench of the Supreme Court ordered the Government to implement the 1991 order, by June 30, 2001. Acting on the directives of the apex court, General Musharraf had set up the Law Ministry Task Force, and a Commission on the Transformation of the Financial

System (CTFS), to look into the Islamisation of economy.[52] The Government Order of June 30, 2000 read, "The Government is determined to eliminate *riba* (interest) from the financial system by June 30, 2001. It appeared that the PML-Q Government was committed to Islamising the economy and all fiscal laws in consonance with the Holy Quran and the Sunnah. It required transforming all fiscal laws, whether relating to the government, commercial banking or foreign transactions, in accordance with the provisions of the *Sharia*."[53] The government also released some reports on the issue.[54] Qazi Hussain Ahmed in an interview claimed, "There is no problem in introducing a *riba*-free economy. All we have to do is implement those reports."[55]

Land Reforms

Since 1947, the feudal lords in Pakistan have accumulated fortunes in partnership with the civil-Military oligarchy and thwarted any land reform initiatives that have been taken up under different regimes. T. Shreedhar says, "According to Census of Agriculture 1990, in Punjab province only one per cent landowners possess 26 per cent of the total cultivable land which is 26.6 million acres. Few from this class can actually be defined as growers and tillers as they are all feudal lords employing landless farmers and keeping them as serfs."[56] Influential feudals have played a dominant role in politics and benefited for backing one or the other party in elections. Twice, the government tried to introduce land reforms—in 1959 (under Ayub Khan) and 1972 (under Z.A. Bhutto), but it did not have any major effect.[57] The MMA manifesto provided for 'the abolishment of all chronic and new feudal system with forfeiture of illegal wealth and its distribution among poor; and to provide lands to peasants and farmers for the livelihood and guarantee reasonable prices to their produce.'[58] The Pakistan Awami Tehriq (PAT) party maintained, "Feudalism and sardari as a system will be totally abolished, and absentee landlordism banned. Through a process of land reforms excess lands of over 50 acres per family will be taken over by the State without compensation, and a minimum of 8 acres will be given to the landless tenants on easy terms. This will result in immense increase in agricultural production and will raise the standard of living of the rural population (which is 70 per cent of the total population) to a great extent. It will give a tremendous boost to the country's economy as well." [59]

The World Bank also put forward a proposal in a report on land reforms in Pakistan to raise agricultural productivity, reduce rural poverty and realize the full potential of economic growth. According to the report, 2 per cent of households own more than 40 acres of land and control 44 per cent of the land area. Collectively, large and very large farmers control 66 per cent of all agricultural land.[60] Different governments over the years have distributed state lands among the landless peasants, but at a very slow pace.[61] Qazi Hussain Ahmed, in an interview to *Dawn* had announced, "MMA would disband all the Jagirdaris (big land ownerships) and carry out fresh land reforms to put a limit to land holdings in the country.[62] This can be regarded as one aspect of the MMA's agenda which has more positive fallouts than negative. It would play a key role in alleviating poverty and hardship in the rural areas, where the feudals and landowners would not no longer be able to exploit the tenants. The only challenge would be getting such a legislation passed in the National Assembly where influential feudals and Jagirdars may use their political clout and power to block any such measure, which may impinge on their privileges.

Educational Reforms

The stand of the MMA remains a cause of concern as the party issued a range of recommendations for Pakistan's educational system based on the implementation of *Sharia* which among other issues, included segregation of female students in educational institutions. In December 2002, the MMA organised a convention for women, to dispel fears of imposition of a Taliban-like code for women. At the convention, Qazi Hussain Ahmed said that while the MMA would give equal job opportunities to women, repeal discriminatory laws, and abolish honour killings, the party would also ban co-education and establish separate educational institutions for women. [63] He said, "The country, because of its defence and debt liabilities, already has very little to spend on education, and the effort should be to make maximum use of the limited money available".[64] The justification for these recommendations seemed economically very unconvincing and one can put a counter Argument saying that if there were financial constraints in the educational sector, then there was all the more need not to undertake these measures. Segregation of educational institutions would certainly entail more expenses for altering the existing infrastructure. Interestingly, the banning of co-education was not part of the MMA's manifesto and turned out to be the party's hidden agenda. In one instance, after being questioned in an interview Qazi Hussain Ahmed diplomatically responded, "We haven't said that we'll take the girls out tomorrow. This is a gradual plan. When separate arrangements have been arranged, we'll implement it. This is not the MMA's demand but a demand of our women. Most women skip education because they do not like studying in co-educational institutions. And there are no alternative arrangements. What we spend on education is shameful."[65] The educational sector in Pakistan will come under increasing pressure from the MMA which would seek to enforce the *Sharia* socially if the legislative option fails to materialise. The informal policing of the streets by the MMA's foot-soldiers, to enforce the Islamic code of conduct, does not wait for any legislative sanction and primarily draws its strength from the fear factor and its self-righteous image.

Curbs on Non-Governmental Organizations (NGOs)

The Islamist parties have been vociferously opposed to the workings of the NGOs in the province. The MMA called for streamlining NGOs and charged them for using foreign funds and promoting the interests of other countries. It also alleged that many NGOs were indulging in espionage and hurting Pakistani culture. It may be noted that the MMA was critical of the NGOs that vehemently opposed child labour in the football industry of Pakistan. The party's stand was that only those NGOs that help provide children with education, vocational training, and health services and create conditions for better income for families, will be encouraged. NGOs, especially in NWFP and Balochistan have come under immense pressure. Hafiz Hashmat said, "The activities of NGOs will have to be monitored because of grassroot concerns about a hidden agenda that could undermine Islamic values and cultural traditions."[66] The curbs on NGOs could be a very detrimental blow to Pakistan's development initiatives, as they play an important role in providing necessary services in education, health, and other sectors, which compensates for government's failure. After imposing curbs on NGOs, the MMA will have to provide alternative services, else their popularity may suffer a beating, from those who have been supported by the NGOs.

Stoking Anti-US and Anti-West Sentiments

The MMA vociferously condemned US policies in Afghanistan and its aggression against Iraq. Anti-Americanism and General Musharraf's pro-US tilt following the September 11 attacks can be considered the determining factors in bringing the six-party alliance together. Although the MMA was formed in June 2002, at Aghora Khattak in NWFP, much before the US campaign started against the Taliban in 2002, the US attack on Afghanistan gave the MMA a burning political issue to be exploited in its election campaigns.[67] Anti-US feeling intensified in Pakistan from mid-2002, after a *madarassa* was bombed in Angoor Adda, inside Pakistan, in an exchange of fire between a Pakistani soldier and the US troops. Subsequently, as the war in Afghanistan progressed, tightening the noose squeezing the Taliban regime, killing scores of Taliban fighters, mostly Pukhtuns, the hate-wave in Pakistan began to intensify. The anti-US sentiments also gained momentum after the US Immigration and Naturalization Service (INS) arrested and deported over 1,200 Pakistani immigrants to Pakistan in the post-9/11 security roundup. According to the National Council of Pakistani Americans (NCPA), another 167 cases of deportation are pending in the US courts and as per the estimates up to two lakh Pakistanis are in the loop, which may result in the deportation of at least 50,000. The Pakistani courts were helpless in providing any relief in the matter. Many Pakistanis reportedly sold off their assets in the US and moved to Canada. The interference of the US and its forces and the intelligence agencies inside Pakistan did not auger well with the public which was exploited by the MMA. Qazi Hussain Ahmed said, "FBI has been given a free hand to conduct raids on any house, mosque or *madaris* and round up respectable citizens while Pakistani courts are helpless in offering any relief."[68]

Another issue that added to the ire of people against the US was the National Security Entry/Exit Registration System (NSEERS). The re-registration requirement required aliens (read foreigners) to re-register after 30 days and one year of continuous presence in the United States. NSEERS was first mooted by the Department of Justice and then the Department of Homeland Security (DHS) in compliance with the Congressional directive for a comprehensive entry-exit programme by 2005. The controversial part though was that, out of 25 countries included in the list to conform to NSEERS requirements namely Afghanistan, Algeria, Bahrain, Bangladesh, Egypt, Eritrea, Indonesia, Iran, Iraq, Jordan, Kuwait, Libya, Lebanon, Morocco, North Korea, Oman, Pakistan, Qatar, Somalia, Saudi Arabia, Sudan, Syria, Tunisia, United Arab Emirates, and Yemen, 23 were Muslim countries. In December 2003, although the DHS decided to suspend NSEERS, but it was a little late in the day and the damage had already been done.[69] Many sections in Pakistan ascribed anti-US sentiments to be a catalyst for the rise of Islamist parties. The former Information Minister Mushahid Hussain wrote, "It can be said that the election results are the first direct reaction against America's anti-Islam policies".[70] The Urdu daily *Jang* reported, "The success of the MMA reflects the sentiments of the Pakistani people against America's anti-Islam policies. The people of Pakistan now want bold changes in the country's foreign policies."[71] Much of the anti-American sentiments in the present context germinated in Pakistan following the US attack on Afghanistan and overthrow of the Taliban regime after September 11 and it intensified further as the US troops entered Iraq against the Saddam Hussein regime. The MMA mobilised more and more support against the US' campaign and its Punjab unit chief, Hafiz Idris, organised a massive anti-US demonstration indicating that that the party was considering sending its youth to fight against the US in Iraq, as they once did against the Soviets in Afghanistan. On behalf of the MMA he also demanded that the all US forces including the FBI personnel reportedly carrying out raids against the Al-Qaida militants, hiding inside Pakistan, must leave immediately.[72] Maulana Shah Ahmad Noorani, Nawabzada Nasarullah Khan, Fazl-ur Rehman, Qazi Hussain Ahmed, and Javed Hashmi are in the long list of prominent leaders who warned the US of serious consequences for its policies in Iraq, Afghanistan and Pakistan. In reaction to the US attack on Iraq in 2003, the MMA organized 'million-man-march' in Karachi (March 1), Rawalpindi (March 9), and Lahore (March 23), Peshawar (March 30), Quetta (April 2) and Multan (April 4). The MMA also observed March 28 as a countrywide protest day against the US invasion of Iraq.[73] These marches reported massive attendance by activists even from the moderate parties, several non-political organizations including a large number of women. In Lahore, an estimated 2,00,000 people had turned up on the streets for the cause. Pakistan echoed with strong anti-US sentiments which made General Musharraf's involvement in the global war against terrorism very complicated and his predicaments became clearly visible when he said, "We can talk to the US...but how can we convince them on our points when the whole country echoes with the slogans of jihad (against the US)".[74] The MMA's ideological orientations emanating from its anti-West became the biggest hindrance to US-Pakistan relations, and remain to be so. The Congressional Research Service Report mentioned the US as being watchful of these developments while continuing with its engagement with General Musharraf in the global war against terrorism.[75]

Conclusion

Pakistan's support to the US-led forces in the overthrow of the Taliban regime in Afghanistan and US pressure on General Musharraf to clamp down the protesting jihadis in Pakistan generated strong anti-US sentiments across Pakistan. The MMA called for a unified response against the US and the West and Jihad became the catalyst for uniting the *Ummah*. Although, it perplexed many as to why was the MMA waging an offensive against General Musharraf considering the valuable support he had rendered to the party in the 2002 elections. One possible explanation could be that the MMA, after being 'betrayed' by General Musharraf on the uniform issue, had to take corrective measures, short of capsizing the regime, to resurrect its public image. Likewise, to soothe their tempers General Musharraf also avoided any direct confrontation by ignoring the Islamisation drive in the province. It was a convenient policy for both sides to be allowed necessary political space to each other without breaking out from the relationship. Besides, the presence of a strong Islamist constituency in Pakistan's political spectrum provided General Musharraf with a card to present before the US whenever necessary as the unavoidable alternative, should he exit the scene. Nonetheless, one finds a thin line between political machinations and blunders which General Musharraf unfortunately ignored in his power pursuits. It not only seriously damaged Pakistan's standing within the international community, but it opened up a Pandora's box for Pakistan in the years to come. How far would General Musharraf be able to roll back the juggernaut and their extreme agenda became another interesting subject for study. The next chapter looks into the political consequences of the Military-MMA partnership on democracy and the problems it created for General Musharraf. The chapter also explains why and how the Military and the Islamists managed their occasional confrontations to mutual advantage.

NOTES

1. See Ashutosh Misra, "Rise of Islamist parties in Pakistan: Causes and Prospects", *Strategic Analysis*, Vol. 27, No. 2, April-June 2003, p. 210.
2. Interview (in New Delhi) with Major-General (Retd.) Jamshed Ayaz Khan, Director-General Institute for Regional Studies (IRS), Islamabad. March 13, 2005.
3. "Slogans" at http://www.mma.org.pk/campaign/2002/slogans
4. The Urdu daily '*Nawa-i-Waqt*' and '*Din*' reported on the passing of the *Sharia* Bill and its fallout. For the Urdu translation of the reports see "Back to Friday as Holiday: Nuggets from the Urdu Press", March 3, 2003, at http://www.thefridaytimes.com/nuggets.htm.

5. Owais Tohid, "Backward March", *Newsline*, July 2003, p. 24.
6. For analysis see Khaled Ahmed, "Will Qazi Hussain Ahmed Stop Basant Next Year?" at www.thefridaytimes.com/main31.htm. Also see 'MPA for Ban on Basant' at http://www.dawn.com/2003/02/04/nat14.htm
7. Mohammed Riaz, "NWFP PA Passes the Hasbah Bill", at http://www.dawn.com/2005/07/15/top1.htm
8. Iqbal Khattak, "MMA Takes Unconstitutional Step with Sharia, Hisbah Bills" at http://www.thefridaytimes.com/inews6a.htm
9. Zakir Hassnain, "Opposition Calls Hisbah Martial Law of Mullas" at http://www.dailytimes.com.pk/default.asp?page=story_27-8-2003_pg7_27
10. "Pakistan: The Mullahs and the Military", International Crisis Group (ICG) Asia Report No. 49, March 20, 2003, pp. 29-30.
11. "State of Democracy Report", July 1, 2004-September 30, 2004, Pakistan Institute for Legislative Development and Transparency (PILDAT), p. 19.
12. Nasir Iqbal, "Hasba Clauses Ruled Contrary to Constitution: NWFP Governor may not Assent to Law: SC" at http://www.dawn.com/2005/08/05/top1.htm
13. Owais Tohid, "Backward March", *Newsline*, July 2003, p. 27.
14. Mohammed Riaz, "NWFP Adopts Islamic Morality Bill: Opposition Calls it Maulvi's Martial Law", at http://www.dawn.com/2006/11/14/top1.htm
15. Ibid.
16. Nasir Iqbal, "SC Moved Against Hasba Bill", at http://www.dawn.com/2006/11/16/top9.htm.
17. Waseem Ahmed, "MMA MPA Seeks Law Against Music, Women's Photos in Ads.", at http://www.dawn.com/2005/02/04/top7.htm
18. Owais Tohid, 'The Sound of Silence', *Newsline*, July 2003, p. 23.
19. Ibid, p. 24
20. Raja Asghar, "MMA joins Govt Against Bill" at http://www.dawn.com/2005/03/02/top1.htm
21. Veena Kukreja, *Contemporary Pakistan. Political Processes, Conflicts and Crises*, Sage Publications, New Delhi, 2003, p. 172.
22. Naeem Shakeer, "The Blasphemy Law in Pakistan and its Impact" at http://www.ahrchk.net/hrsolid/mainfile.php/1999vol09no07/1143/
23. "Enforcement of Shari'ah Act 1991". Gazette of Pakistan,

Extraordinary, Part I, June 18, 1991, at http://www.pakistani.org/pakistan/legislation/1991/actXof1991.html

24. "Noorani Asks for Restoration of 1973 Constitution", at www. mma.org. pk/news/2002/10/Noorani.restoration.Constitu tion.Islamic.identity.country.shtml
25. Ghani Chaudhary, "Women in Pak Elections", at http://www.dailymirror.lk/2002/10/16/opinion/3.html.
26. ICG Asia Report, No. 49. p. 21.
27. Ibid., p. 24.
28. "JI to Give Women Military Training", at http://www.mma.org.pk/news/2002/10/JI
29. Veena Kukreja, 2003, p. 172.
30. Zakir Hassnain, "NWFP PA Rejects Amendments to Hudood Ord" at http://www.dailytimes.com.pk/default.asp?page=story_10-9-2003_pg7_8
31. "MMA Women MNAs Oppose Change to Hudood Ordinance" at http://www.dailytimes.com.pk/default.asp?page=story_10-9-2003_pg7_31
32. Shaukat Piracha, "PPPP Moves NA to Repeal Hudood Ord", at http://www.dailytimes.com.pk/default.asp?page=story_16-10-2003_pg1_5
33. "Qazi Sets Terms for Cooperation: PM Promises No Repeal of Hudood Law" at http://www.dawn.com/2004/03/10/nat3.htm
34. "Hudood Laws will be Amended, and not Repealed" at http://www.dawn.com/2006/07/18/top7.htm
35. Mukhtar Mai (meaning elder sister) was gang-raped on the orders of the council of tribal elders in June 2002 in the Meerwala village in Pakistan's Punjab province. For no fault of her's Mai was subjected to the gang-rape by four amidst a cheering crowd when her 14 year old brother was allegedly found moving with a girl of a rival clan in the village. After hearing of her brother's trial, she pleaded for mercy and so the council of elders instead ordered her to be raped as a compensation for the family of the rival clan. Mai has ever since attracted world-wide support against the injustice which has been imposed upon her by the laws of tribes in Punjab province. It was her grit to fight for justice against her perpetrators and the tribal code of 'justice' that allowed such grouse injustice against her that she got four of the culprits punished. The book,

In the Name of Honour: A Memoir (Atria Books, 2006) which provides an emotional and moving tale of her horrific experience is translated into English by Marie Therese Cuny.

Dr. Shazia Khalid's rape case can be considered as one of the far-reaching and serious cases that Pakistan has witnessed. A 32 year-old medical doctor, Dr. Khalid was employed with the government-owned Pakistan Petroleum Limited in a large gas facility in Sui, Balochistan. In January 2005, as per press reports she was raped by Captain Hamad of the Defence Security Guards, which is a part of the Pakistani Military and responsible for the security of the complex at Sui where Dr. Khalid lived. Initially, General Musharraf had given Captain Hamad a clean chit saying that he was 100 percent innocent, but later he was arrested and now an independent inquiry is conducted into the case and Captain Hamad is undergoing DNA and others tests. In January 2005, the Governor of Balochistan Awais Ahmed Ghani made a statement on record that Captain Hamad would be punished if found guilty. The inquiry is underway at the moment.

36. Raja Ashgar, "Some Respite for Women, at Last: Protection of Rights Bill lets through NA", at http://www.dawn.com/2006/11/16/top1.htm
37. Raja Ashgar, "Senate Passes Women's Bill; MMA Amendments Rejected", at http://www.dawn.com/2006/11/24/top1.htm
38. Ahmed Hassan, "MMA to 'Resign' in December", at http://www.dawn.com/2006/11/17/top3.htm
39. "Resignation not the Only Option, Says Fazl", at http://www.dawn.com/2006/11/28/top7.htm
40. Bahzad Alam Khan, "MMA in Do-or-die Talks", at http:www.dawn.com/2006/12/07/top2.htm
41. "Shujaat Rady for Talks with MMA Leaders", at http://www.dawn.com/2006/11/20/top3.htm
42. Ghafar Ali, "Centre has Lifted Ban on Madrassa Registration" at http://www.dailytimes.com.pk/default.asp?page=story_25-7-2004_pg7_36
43. Mohammad Imran, "Centre Planning Law to Register Seminaries" at www.dailytimes.com.pk/default. asp?page=story_28-2-2005_pg1_3
44. Ibid.

45. Hasan Mansoor, "Barelvi-Deobandi Fissure Over MMA Proposal", *Friday Times*, September 3-9, 2004, p. 4.
46. "Madrassa Registration to be discussed at NSC" at http://www.dailytimes.com.pk/default.asp?page=story_24-2-2005_pg1_7
47. Amir Siddiqui, "Passport Controversy", *Newsline*, Annual 2005, p. 53
48. Syed Irfan Raza, "Nadra to Issue Passports with Religion from Today", at http://www.dawn.com/2005/03/28/top3.htm
49. See Appendix IV.
50. Veena Kukreja, 2003, p. 171.
51. Zakir Hassnain, "PM to Open BoK Islamic Banking Branch Tomorrow" at http://www.dailytimes.com.pk/default.asp?page=story_21-11-2003_pg7_38
52. B. Raman, "Islamisation of Pakistan's Economy", September 30, 2000, at http://www.asiafeatures.com/business/0010,1505,03.html.
53. Ibid.
54. Zafarullah Haq Committee, State Bank of Pakistan, and Council of Islamic Ideology (CII) have so far compiled the report on economic reforms.
55. M. Ilyas Khan, "Interview with Qazi Hussain Ahmed", *Herald*, November 2002, p. 56.
56. T. Sreedhar, "Pakistan's Economic Dilemma", June 18, 1998, at http://www.nyu.edu/globalbeat/southasia/06181998sreedhar1.html
57. M. Abul Fazal, "Feudalism", *The Nation* (Lahore). June 10 & 11,1997, cited in Veena Kukreja, 2003, p. 81.
58. See Appendix IV.
59. Safdar Hasan Siddiqi, "Building Quaid-e-Azam's Pakistan", at http://www.insaf.org.pk/articles/articles_building_Quaid-e-Azams_Pakistan.htm
60. *Poverty in Pakistan: Vulnerabilities, Social Gaps, and Rural Dynamics.* World Bank Report. No. 24296. October 28, 2002.
61. Jawaid Bokhari, "World Bank for Land Reforms", at http://www.dawn.com/2002/11/13/ebr4.htm.
62. "MMA Vows to Carry out Land Reforms", at http://www.mma.org.pk/news/2002/10/mma.ows.carry.out.land.reforms.shtml

63. "Freedom of Voice" at http://www.dawn.com/2002/10/22ed.htm
64. *Ibid.*
65. M. Ilyas Khan, 2002, p. 58.
66. ICG Asia Report. No. 49, p. 30.
67. M. Ilyas Khan, "Inside the MMA", *Herald.* November 2002. p. 46.
68. "3 States on US Hit-list After Iraq says Qazi", at www.dailymailnews.com/sep2002/25/main/?news=7. Also see, 'Pakistan Next on US Hit list', at http://www.jamaat.org/news/pr021203.html.
69. "If Iraq is Attacked, Can We be Far Behind, Ask Pakistanis" at www.navakal.com/news/regional/200212236009.asp Also see press release Fact Sheet: Changes to National Security Entry/Exit Registration System, Department of Homeland Security, December 1, 2003 at http://www.dhs.gov/dhspublic/display?content=3020
70. Mushahid Hussain's piece in *Nawa-e-Waqt,* October 15, 2002, cited in Shiraz Zia, 'Media', *Herald.* November 2002. p. 26.
71. *Jang,* October 12, 2002, *Ibid.*
72. "MMA to Send Youth to Iraq to Fight Against US", at http://www.thenation.co.uk/kash.html.
73. Amjad Mehmood, "MMA Marchers Condemn Attack", at http://www.dawen.com/2003.03/24/top3.htm.
74. "The Net Closes on Pakistan", at www.pakistan-facts.com/article.php?story=20030122091532637.
75. K. Alan Kronstadt, *Pakistan's Domestic Political Developments: Issues for Congress.* Congressional Research Service Report for Congress. June 19, 2003. p. CRS-6.

CHAPTER IV

Military-MMA Alliance
Marriage of Convenience

The marriage between the Military and the Muttahida-Majlis-e-Amal (MMA) emerged out of their political impediments, common challenges and quest for more power. It was an alliance which was based on political opportunism and compulsion and therefore susceptible to confrontation right from its inception. Yet, given their opposing views on many counts how they managed to cooperate for over four years is the central theme of this chapter. This chapter presents an account of how General Pervez Musharraf tried to make the best of his ties with the MMA and how such political expediency brought their relationship to a breaking point.

General Musharraf was keen to create an alternative political force to sideline the PPPP and the PML-N, the MMA on its part was eager to undo its image of being merely a 'street power' and transform itself into a viable political power. The run-up to the elections and the contemporary factors made the scenario conducive for both sides to exploit. General Musharraf was capitalizing on the public widespread disenchantment with Benazir Bhutto and Nawaz Sharif for having failed to deliver the goods between 1988 and 1999. Scenes of people celebrating the overthrow of Nawaz Sharif in 1999 with drums and sweets emboldened General Musharraf enormously and encouraged him to expel the two leaders out of Pakistan without causing any public outcry. In the light of the long history of political convergence of interests between the Islamists and the Military, the MMA felt encouraged when General Pervez Musharraf came to power in 1999. The foundation of a long term political understanding was laid when General Musharraf turned to various jehadi groups for support during April 2002 Presidential Referendum. As expected Jihadi groups played a vital part in organising meetings, campaigning and mobilising public support for General Musharraf. Their logistical and operational services had a big influence in moulding General Musharraf's approach towards them. Before the elections, various Jihadi outfits joined different Islamist parties, with most joining the Jamaat-e-Ulem-Islam (F). After the MMA was launched as a political party comprising six-different parties, the election commission approved of their madrassa degrees as equivalent of a university graduate degree. General Musharraf also facilitated the dropping of pending cases against several MMA leaders. In addition, a range of factors discussed in the previous chapter brought the MMA to power in an unprecedented fashion. It heralded a phase in Pakistan's political history wherein both, the Military and the Islamists, obliged each other with political favours and constantly worked on consolidating their respective positions in the political spectrum.

Legal Framework Order (LFO) 2002

The LFO was mooted by General Musharraf in August 2002, to bring changes in the 1973 Constitution, before the 2002 general elections were held. The aim was to strengthen the hold over power both as President and Army Chief. The April 30, 2002 'doctored' Referendum had already given him the much-needed 'legitimacy' as President for five years, and after October 2002 to institutionally entrench himself further, he required to induct the LFO into the Constitution.

Initially, the opposition including the MMA, gave General Musharraf a tough time in the National Assembly and the echoes of 'No LFO', 'go General Musharraf go' became a regular feature.[1] It demanded that the LFO should have the approval of the Parliament to be incorporated into the Constitution. General Musharraf argued that there was no need for any parliamentary approval as the Supreme Court had validated his coup and empowered him to amend the Constitution.[2]

Unable to reach a compromise with the opposition (minus the MMA), the government began parleys with the MMA in July 2003 till November. When the dialogue resumed in December, the MMA set a deadline of December 18 for introducing the amendments in the Constitution and at the same time started demonstration on the streets against the government's stand on the LFO.[3]

Finally the 'deal' over the LFO was signed on December 24, 2003 [4] between the government and the MMA and on that basis the 17th Amendment was passed in the National Assembly and the Senate on December 30, 2003 by a two-third majority, and signed by the President on December 31, 2003.[5]

The opposition parties including the PPPP, the PML-N and other smaller parties like the Pashtoon-Khwa Milli Awami Party (PkMAP), Awami National Party (ANP), and Jamhoori Wattan Party (JWP) had boycotted the voting. The 'deal' created a huge wedge between the MMA and rest of the opposition.[6] The ARD expressed its dismay over the deal and severely criticized MMA for betraying the opposition and siding with General Musharraf.[7] The 17th Amendment introduced changes in 9 Articles on the following lines:

1. The President would retain the power to dissolve the National Assembly at his discretion but he would submit the dissolution decision to the Supreme Court for scrutiny and adjudication within 15 days of the dissolution;
2. The National Security Council (NSC) would be set up by ordinary legislation in the Parliament;
3. The President will appoint the Chiefs of the three Services of the armed forces and Chairman, Joint Chiefs of Staff Committee in consultation with the Prime Minister;
4. The local government ordinances will be removed from the Constitution's 6th Schedule in December 2009;
5. Three-year extension in the retirement age of the judges of the Supreme Court and High Courts would be withdrawn;
6. The President, General Musharraf would seek a vote of confidence from the members present and voting in each house separately, and;

7. He could not combine Presidency with the office of Army Chief beyond December 31, 2004[8]

Notwithstanding the charges levied by the opposition regarding the deal, the MMA defended its decision saying that it was done in the larger interests of democracy. Maulana Hafiz Hussain Ahmed, the MMA deputy parliamentary leader said, "General Musharraf had confessed that approval of 17th Amendment was not a matter of loss or win for any party and had promised with the nation to take off uniform by December 31."[9] He added that if the President reneged from his promise to take off the uniform, the MMA would launch a nation-wide protest against him. The Deputy Secretary General of the MMA, Liaquat Baloch said that the passing of the 17th Amendment was done through constitutional means and it is a victory for the party since it managed to table it in the Parliament for discussion. He added that MMA still has some reservations over some clauses such as the local government ordinance, police order, and ordinances about education and industries and these would be settled through consultation by the committee set up by the Prime Minister.[10] The MMA was rewarded for facilitating the 'deal'. Maulana Fazl-ur Rehman was 'declared' leader of the opposition in the National Assembly on May 25, 2005 causing a controversy. The MMA secured the position by showing the support of 68 legislators, whereas the plea of ARD candidate, Makdoom Amin Fahim, with the backing of 80 legislators was turned down by the Speaker on the ground that the ARD parties did not form part of a single political entity, unlike the MMA. Makdoom Fahim reacted strongly saying that it is political dishonesty of the highest order and there was no question of cooperation with the MMA because it had supported the government.[11] As the leader of the opposition, Fazl-ur Rehman also became a member of the NSC which suited General Musharraf's political scheme. Incidentally, Fazl-ur Rehman's father, Maulana Mufti Mahmood, was also leader of the opposition from 1973 to 1977 during Zulfiqar Ali Bhutto's regime.[12] The establishment also gave respite to the MMA by not raking up the issue of the MMA members not having recognized graduate degrees. The Centre has been considerate to the NWFP and its interests and largely ignored the

Islamization currently underway there. The MMA cadres have been spared of hot pursuit in the wake of the global war against terrorism (GWT).

Vote of Confidence in the National Assembly

Having succeeded in getting the 17th Amendment through, General Musharraf turned to securing parliamentary legitimacy through a simple majority vote of confidence. In the pre-December 31, 2003 Constitution no such provision for a vote of confidence existed. In order to get the required votes with little difficulty, he threw a bait as well saying that he would relinquish his uniform on December 31, 2004. The voting was held on January 1, 2004 in the National Assembly, the Senate and the four provincial assemblies. General Musharraf secured a simple majority of 658 votes (just above 56 percent in the 1,170-strong electoral college) of the 342-seat National Assembly, the 100-seat Senate and 728 members of the four provincial assemblies.[13] The Chief Election Commissioner Irshad Hasan Khan declared "General Musharraf, the President in office, having received a majority of votes of members present and voting of both the houses of parliament and provincial assemblies as per paragraph 18 of the Second Schedule to the Constitution of the Islamic Republic of Pakistan is hereby declared elected in terms of Clause (8) of Article 41 of the Constitution..."[14]

The MMA's 'non-participatory' strategy facilitated General Musharraf's political machination, yet again and abstained from voting without opposing him. A helpless ARD was left shouting anti-Musharraf slogans throughout the proceedings and eventually boycotting the vote as well. From the MMA's decision it appeared that it was a conscious policy to abstain from voting and not to be seen as an active player in General Musharraf's whole scheme and thus avoid any blame-sharing without rocking the process itself.

Twin Hats

Undoubtedly, one of the most daunting decisions of General Musharraf has been his decision to continue as Army Chief beyond the December 31, 2004 deadline. The pre-December 2003 Constitution disallowed any Army Chief to hold any other office of profit. The Article [63(1)d] implied that the President cannot hold any other office of profit in the service of Pakistan. However, it allowed Parliament to exclude any government assignment from the category by ordinary legislation.[15] The Cabinet announced on September 15, 2004 that Pervez Musharraf is likely to retain the post of Army Chief after December 31, 2004 and there were no constitutional restriction on him remaining in uniform.[16] The Information Minister Sheikh Rashid Ahmed said that the 17th Amendment provided for General Musharraf holding two posts simultaneously.[17] The announcement came after the breakaway group of the PPPP, the PPP-Patriot expressed their willingness to see Pervez Musharraf continue as the Army Chief to ensure political stability.

The Punjab Assembly was the first to table the resolution to support his continuation as Army Chief. On September 13, 2004 the Punjab Assembly passed the resolution supporting General Musharraf on the uniform issue.[18] However, two days later, on September 15, 2004 the NWFP Assembly passed a resolution against General Musharraf's continuation as Army Chief after December 2004, with 55 votes in favour and 14 against.[19] A politically betrayed MMA took a firm position against General Musharraf. The resolution witnessed a similar fate in the Balochistan Assembly. The MMA expressed its reservations against the resolution and due to lack of support the treasury withdrew the resolution on September 20, 2004, to avoid embarrassment in case the resolution was defeated.[20] In Sindh, where the MQM is in coalition with the PML-Q the resolution was passed on September 22, 2004.[21] Eventually, 'President to Hold Another Office Bill 2004' was passed on October 14, 2004 in the National Assembly allowing General Musharraf to continue as Army Chief after December 2004[22], and in the Senate amid protests.[23]

The opposition labeled the move as 'illegal' and 'unconstitutional'.[24] The reneging of General Musharraf from his 'promise' caused serious damage to the credibility of the MMA which was at loss of words to express its dismay over the betrayal. Hafiz Hussain Ahmed, the MMA's deputy in the National Assembly said that in the light of the pledge and the televised address made before the public in December 2003, Musharraf is bound to quit the post of army chief.[25] Since then the wedge between the MMA and General Musharraf began to widen and the former realized in retrospect that it was political hara-kiri to support General Musharraf at the cost of its own credibility and democracy.

National Security Council (NSC)

The LFO provided for the setting up of a National Security Council through simple legislation. The bill for this purpose was moved by the government on April 2, 2004 in the National Assembly, where it was strongly opposed by the opposition. This time the MMA also, reversing its supporting stand, opposed the bill. The opposition walked out and the National Assembly's Standing Committee passed the bill in merely 35 minutes on April 7, 2004.[26] The bill was passed in the Senate on April 14, 2004 amidst uproar.[27] The PPPP parliamentary leader Raza Rabbani lamented the act saying, "Today's incident—this is a tragedy—is the worst in the history of Pakistan's Parliament and Senate."[28] MMA's parliamentary leader in the Senate Khurshid Ahmed labeled it as a "national insecurity bill".[29] The President signed the bill on April 19, 2004 and Prime Minister Zafarullah Jamali hailed the creation of the NSC observing that it will check presidential powers to dissolve the National Assembly and serve as 'a safety valve to the democratic system in the country',[30] though it did little to soothe the opposition's tempers.

The NSC with a total strength of 13 (including the chairman) is composed of the President who would also be Chairman; Prime Minister; Chairman of the Senate; Leader of the Opposition in the National Assembly; four provincial Chief Ministers; Chairman, Joint Chiefs of Staff Committee; and the Service Chiefs. The NSC Secretariat is headed by a Secretary appointed by the President. The broad functions of the NSC include:

A. To serve as forum for consultation to the President and the government on matters of national security, including the sovereignty, integrity, defence, security of the state and crisis management.[31]

B. To formulate and make recommendation to the President and the government in accordance with the consultations on above.[32]

The rights and mandate of the NSC left little doubt that its primary purpose was to provide an institutional and constitutional backing to Military's dominance and supremacy in Pakistan. Feeling the need to counter popular objections to the purpose and intent of the NSC, General Musharraf in his address in the NSC meeting on June 24, 2004 declared that the NSC was not above the Parliament and that it will "serve as a check on the office of the President...(It) would avert imposition of martial law in the future"..."if the NSC rejects the views of the army chief, then he (would) not be able to impose the martial law".[33] However, General Musharraf's justification behind creating the NSC is invalidated considering its composition of this supranational body. It includes the President as the Chairman, who was also the Army Chief. Then there are Chairman Joint Chief of the Staff Committee and the three Service Chiefs. In the present context, how can the NSC possibly reject the views of the Army Chief who is also the Chairman, by virtue of being the President and also has a supporting presence of his fellow servicemen in the NSC. In case of a non-Army Chief being the President, given the history of civil-Military relations in Pakistan, the President would rarely act against the wishes of the Army Chief. For similar reasons, the Prime Minister would also fall in line and the four provincial Chief Ministers be more concerned the their respective government's survival. Therefore, it would be apt to label the NSC as a tool of the Military, for the Military, and by the Military.

A segment within the MMA has been sternly opposed to the NSC in principle. The NWFP Chief Minister Akram Khan Durrani and Maulana Fazl-ur Rehman, though boycotted the initial NSC meetings, they were willing to reconsider their decision due to the latter's proximity with General Musharraf. On the other hand, Qazi Hussain Ahmed was opposed to Fazl-ur Rehman and Akram Khan Durrani attending the NSC meeting, whereas JUI-S, Ahle Hadith and Pakistan Islami Tehrik were in favour of attending the meeting. Not surprisingly, the NWFP general council of the MMA condoned the continuous boycott of the NSC meetings by the two leaders (Durrani and Rehman), finding it detrimental to the interests of the province.[34] Fazl-ur Rehman was reluctant to allow Akram Khan Durrani to attend the meeting primarily because of Qazi Hussain Ahmed's reservations.[35] To avoid any political damage, Maulana Fazl-ur Rehman brought the issue to the Central *Shura* of the party where the final decision was to be taken.[36] Eventually Akra Khan Durrani decided in favour of attending the NSC meeting in October 2005 following the massive earthquake that had rocked Pakistan's northern and north-western areas. Justifying his decision, he said, "I did it for the best interest of the province and the five districts destroyed in the earthquake."[37]

Local Governments

Notwithstanding local government being a non-federal subject, in 2001 General Musharraf introduced the idea of devolution of power and participatory governance at the local, tehsil and district levels through local bodies elections to be held on 'non-party' basis. The larger motive though, apart from increasing the Centre's hold over provincial bureaucracy through the local representatives was to build a network of local influential politicians and workers who could be utilised in campaigning for his party, the PML-Q in the 2007 elections. Like his predecessor Ayub Khan, General Musharraf too, supported the idea of local bodies for creating a support base for himself which would be a substitute for direct democracy. As a result, even if the provincial governments remained hostile to the federal diktats, the Centre could still influence developments and events in the province through the local bodies, representatives and Nazims. It was a parallel executive within the province that would facilitate the Centre's schemes without the support of the provincial government. However, such a scheme had its own limitations as it brought the centre and the province at the collision course. In April 2004, the National Reconstruction Bureau (NRB) stressed on the utility of the system calling it a "break from the status quo",[38] and General Musharraf stated that the local government system "must be supported and strengthened as it would serve as a catalyst for transfer of benefits of macro-economic progress down to the grass root level."[39] Several contradictions required attention to make this system work smoothly. First, the differences over the jurisdiction of powers between the district nazims (equivalent of a Mayor) and the provincial government caused a rift between the two. The bureaucracy was caught in between but eventually chose to abide by the orders of the provincial government, which was more inclined towards obliging the parliamentarians and other well-wishers of the province. Second, disputes surfaced between the parliamentarian and the nazims over the disbursement of development funds. Third, there were many cases of the district council and the nazims differing with each other regarding fund disbursements. And fourth, the political leanings of the nazims also became a problem in the provinces such as Sindh and NWFP where non-favourable governments were in power. The political tug- of-war impeded daily working of the local governments, wherein the political affiliations transformed administrative problems into political tussles.[40]

The powerplay between the provincial government and the nazims assumed such proportions in Balochistan that the latter resorted to hunger strikes and protest marches against the alleged over-bearing influence of the former. In the NWFP, over the non-cooperative attitude of the government and differences over the allocation of developmental funds, in May 2004, fourteen nazims of the union council in Peshawar had resigned.[41] The Durrani government was totally opposed to any interference by the local government in the jurisdiction of powers, transfers and postings of bureaucrats, and distribution of funds. Besides, it did not want any credit to accrue to the local government for any development programme and with the help of a favourable bureaucracy it kept the powers of the nazims under check.[42] The Chief Minister also proposed changes in the local government system, to *inter alia*, institute its accountability.[43]

In the meantime relations between Akram Khan Durrani and Governor Khalilur Rehman, who assumed charge on March 13, 2004, replacing Iftikhar Hussain Shah, began to turn sour.[44] On March 28, 2005 Akram Khan Durrani overruled a decision of the district government and allowed the MMA's proposed 'million man march' on the Grand Trunk Road in Peshawar. The city district council rejected MMA's request to hold the march in Peshawar. The Governor also issued orders that the proposed march should not be allowed to take place on the roads in Peshawar. The provincial government in response citing non-availability of other places decided to finally hold it in Peshawar itself. The issue became a prestige point for the MMA and to show its clout in the province, it summoned the *madaris* across the NWFP to ensure maximum students' participation. An estimated two million people were expected to participate in the march, but surprisingly the turnout fell way short of the expectations. As per the official estimates only 15,000 people participated in the march. It is important to mention that in the rally Maulana Fazl-ur Rehman said that General Musharraf was trying to crush the Islamists at the behest of the US. He declared that no General would be accepted as the next President. He also called for the closure of US bases in Pakistan and criticised General Musharraf for trying to destablise the MMA government.[45] At the same time, the provincial leadership exercised restraint by keeping the tempers of the protestors at bay and did not allow the Governor to intervene on any pretext whatsoever. Akram Khan Durrani also had to convince the Governor that no provincial minister would participate in the march which was appreciated by the latter.[46] Like in the case of the NSC, the MMA is polarised also on the role of local governments. The JI is supportive of the system unlike the JUI-F because it fought the local body elections in Sindh heads the local government in there. JI's presence in the local body is sizeble and they appear to be giving a tough time to the MQM-PML-Q provincial government.[47] The MQM leadership even urged the Centre to ban the JI in the province, alleging that it wanted to make Karachi the base of Al Qaida and Islamic militants. Clearly, the control of the Karachi city government by the JI has become too bitter a pill for the MQM to swallow.[48]

Differences Over FATA Operations

Federally Administered Tribal Areas (FATA) is a collection of seven tribal agencies—South Waziristan, North Waziristan, Kurram, Orakzai, Khyber, Mohmand and Bajaur, with a population of over 3 million people. There are also frontier regions which are attached to the districts of Peshawar, Bannu, Lakki, Tank, Kohat and Dera Ismail Khan. The constitutional status of FATA is enshrined in the Article 246 and 247 of the 1973 Constitution, which allows the area to be administered internally according to the tribal traditions and customs. The federal government has a political agent for FATA who works as a representative and link.[49] Currently, FATA has twelve independent members in the National Assembly, out of which five support the MMA.[50]

FATA came under the spotlight when the Pakistani Military initiated operations in the area to round up suspected foreign militants. The offensive began on October 2, 2003 at Angor Ada but centred primarily in Wana, capital of South Waziristan. The crackdown on Wana began on January 8, 2004, followed by other offensives on February 24, and then between March 18-30, 2004. Since then, the operations have been carried out at periodic intervals.[51] The Centre combined its offensive posture with incentives to win allegiance of the tribesmen. It offered several development projects including schools, hospitals, roads and drinking water supply for FATA, which worked well.[52]

The scheme however, failed to impress the MMA, which has been very critical of the offensives and warned that it may further destabilise the area. A six-member fact-finding team of the MMA parliamentarians went to FATA, but was stopped near Jandola, from entering the area. The MMA legislators warned that the offensive would result into a direct clash between the people and the army, and it would create misunderstanding among the tribesmen and force them to change their allegiance. The MMA even went to the extent of calling the operations 'an agenda of not only the US but India as well'![53] Qazi Hussain Ahmed questioned the government's claims of killing 50 Al Qaida militants in FATA, alleging that they were civilians. He reportedly even offered the government to use MMA's influence on the tribesmen to end the conflict.[54] Fazl-ur Rehman, on the other hand, while admitting the presence of foreigners in the area, put the blame squarely on the establishment for betraying them. He argued that these foreigners were once trained, financed and armed by the Pakistan government against the Soviets. "The trained ones were later called terrorists while the ones who trained them were not bothered", he said.[55] Maulvi Noor Muhammad, a JUI-F member of the National Assembly, and a hardcore supporter of the Taliban said that the MMA rejected the Military operations in Wana.[56] The Urdu dailies including *Nawa-i-Waqt, Ummat, Jasarat, Friday Special, Takbeer, Nida-i-Millat,* and *Islam* also castigated the establishment's volte-face on the erstwhile jehadis.[57]

The government and the MMA have also been at loggerheads on the issue of registration of foreigners in the tribal belt. The Pakistan government proposed that the foreign nationals in the tribal areas needed to register themselves and for this purpose it devised a four-point plan of action which the MMA approved later. The four points were:

First, registration of the foreigners in the tribal areas; second, regarding sectarianism, for which the MMA agreed to take stern action against the *madaris* and mosques fanning sectarianism and terrorism and agreed to keep the use of loudspeakers limited to *azaan* and *Juma khutbas* (Friday prayers); third, the NWFP governor, Members of National Assembly (MNA) from FATA and local elders to hold consultations to initiate commercial and trade activities in Wana, capital of South Waziristan; and fourth, the MMA would render its full cooperation to the federal government in tackling terrorism.[58] It would be fair to say that the MMA articulated its position on the FATA operations very judiciously. It opposed the operations because of the JUI-F's (Pushtun) links with the Taliban in Afghanistan and hence expressed its solidarity with the Pushtun tribesmen targeted in the operations. The fact that the NWFP borders with FATA, the MMA could not afford to remain silent to any development in the vicinity. Its decision to sign the four-point agreement with the government also helped project itself as a moderate political party which was opposed to sectarianism and terrorism.

Locking Horns Over Balochistan Operations

Balochistan's conflict ridden history has seen four insurgencies in 1948, 1958-59, 1962-63 and 1973-77. The Centre's resolve to find a solution through force ended on a sour note every time, facing stiff opposition from the warring tribes, consisting mainly of the *Bugtis* and *Marris*. At present, in Balochistan, the federal government is building a deep sea port in Gwadar with Chinese help and also establishing three army cantonments to keep the provincial assets (mainly to the upcoming port and the Sui Gas Refinery) secured. Not surprisingly, General Musharraf issued a stern warning when the situation flared up in 2005. He warned, "This is not the 1970s...this time they won't know what hit them".[59]

The crisis exploded when a lady doctor Shazia Khalid, employed with the Pakistan Petroleum Limited (PPL) was allegedly raped by one Captain Emad and three others, belonging to the Defence Security Guard (DSG) on January 2, 2005. In retaliation, on January 6, the Baloch National Army (BLA), the front militant organisation of the warring tribes attacked the DSG and Frontier Constabulary (FC) camps in the province and destroyed it. These were followed by more attacks on the Sui Gas Refinery starting January 8 onwards. Amidst continuing attacks, the news of the gangrape of 15 year-old Parveen Mai, added fuel to the fire. In the operations, around 500 DSG personnel, 5,000 FC forces and 2,500 army regulars were deployed, armed with heavy weapons, helicopter gunships and tanks. Another 30,000 troops were on standby on the Pano Aquil and Quetta Cantonments. The *Bugtis* and *Marris* strength were reported around 15,000 and 16,000, respectively.[60] Over 20,000 people fled Dera Bugti for Quetta in the wake of the federal announcement that all settlements within 15 km of Sui Gas Refinery will be cleared. The government also acquired 400 acres for Rs. 90 million outside Manza Ashrali Thal, of the *Kalpa Balkhanis*, who had turned down the offer in 2003 itself.[61]

The federal government also constituted a 38-member parliamentary committee led by PML-Q Chairman Chaudhary Shujaat Hussain, to settle the conflict through political means. Shujaat Hussain is said to have repeatedly urged the government to refrain from seeking a Military solution to the crisis. A sub-committee under Mushahid Hussain was also sent to Balochistan to investigate the rape incidents and finalise a report. Shujaat Hussain and Mushahid Hussain held several rounds of talks with late Nawab Akbar Khan Bugti, former leader of the Jamhoori Watan Party (JWP), Sardar

Ataullah Mengal, President of the Balochistan National Party (BNP) and Nawab Khair Buksh Marri, leader of the *Marri* tribe, but of no avail.[62] The committee's assurances of no further Military operations and consideration of the legitimate demands of the province fell to deaf ears as Akbar Khan Bugti responded, "The battle for Dera Bugti is the battle for the whole of Balochistan."[63]

The Baloch nationalists demanded the withdrawal of the Military and para-military forces from the area; abolition of 584 checkpoints established by the FC in the province; release of detained political workers and withdrawal of cases against them; and cancellation of land allotments made to the Military.[64] The nationalists challenged that the development of the Gwadar Port will bring more outsiders to the province and aggravate the unemployment situation. It is noteworthy that for decades the Balochs have remained on the fringe, devoid of any development benefits and economic compensation that should have been right fully theirs. Around 60 percent of the country's natural gas is mined from Balochistan, in addition to Saindnik copper mines and valuable mineral repositories which are sources of huge revenue for Pakistan. The Balochs believe that yet again they would be left out of the ongoing projects and the benefits would go to the outsiders and the Centre.[65]

In response, General Musharraf expressed his firm support for the projects in the province, and assured the Baloch leaders that the interests of the people would not be ignored. He also assured that the areas from where the minerals are discovered would be given adequate development packages and the genuine rights of the people granted to them. In addition, the seats reserved for Balochistan in the federal services would be increased and enforcement of quotas ensured.[66] The situation in Balochitan has always been a serious issue for the provincial government to handle. It is not surprising therefore that General Musharraf had to face embarrassment when the ruling PML-Q government in Balochistan expressed its displeasure against the military operations and stressed on resolving the problem through political dialogue. The MMA, Coalition partner, severely criticised the plan for new cantonments, and the MMA leader, Hafiz Hussain Ahmed advised the provincial government against seeking military intervention. The MMA leader, Syed Munawwar Hasan, even went to the extent of saying that the military operations are being undertaken at the behest of the US and the cantonments would be used by the US as bases to launch an attack on Iran.[67] The MMA has vociferously opposed the federal government in public, but on record maintained a 'shrewdly wavering' position by keeping silent in the cabinet meetings.[68] Though the MMA advised the provincial government against military intervention, its official stand on the issue has drawn flak from various quarters on the ground that it refused to part with the coalition. The ARD accused the MMA of double standards, saying that the MMA should have withdrawn from the coalition in Balochistan if it was opposed to the government's policies and the military operations in principle.

The situation in the province suddenly exploded when veteran leader Sardar Akbar Khan Bugti, former Chief Minister of Balochistan and leader of the Jamhoori Watan Party (JWP), along with 37 Baloch nationalist was killed in the Chalgri area of Bhamboor hills of Dera Bugti district in a military raid on August 26, 2006. In the raid, 21 security personnel were also killed. According to sources, Nawab Bugti's hideout was ascertained through the satellite tracking system. Helicopter gunships and heavy artillery bombarded the cave where he was holed up completely trapping him and his supporters inside. Federal Minister for Information Muhammad Ali Durrani announced, "Nawab Akbar Khan Bugti was killed in the operation along with some family members".[69] There were reports of his grandsons, Nawabzada Baramdagh Bugti and Nawabzada Aali Bugti also being killed in the operation which was later found to be untrue. It is said they had escaped just before the operation began. Major opposition parties including the PPP and the MMA lambasted the killings, calling for an immediate cessation of the military operations.[70] The killing of Sardar Bugti caused widespread rioting in Balochistan, particularly in Quetta where his supporters burnt government buildings, banks, vehicles and shops. Over 600 rioters were arrested by the Frontier Corps personnel and indefinite curfew imposed in the city. All inbound highways, flights, and trains were cancelled, throwing normal life in the province completely out of gear. In response, General Musharraf said the he would take "every step" to ensure the writ of the government everywhere in the country. He also said the he was open to negotiations with every political entity but was totally intolerant to attacks on the security forces in the region.[71] However, General Musharraf's statement was contrary to what the evidence suggested. In 2005 Chaudhary Shujaat Hussain and Mushahid Hussain, who were part of the parliamentary committee on Balochistan, had held talks with Sardar Bugti and had succeeded in diffusing the crisis to a large extent. It is believed that contrary to the Committee's recommendation of resolving the crisis through talks, General Musharraf acted on the advise of his top military commanders who alleged that Sardar Bugti was the key troublemaker and was operating through foreign support.[72] Jamali Bugti, son of the late Sardar raised a pertinent question that why does the military regime not take action against mobs and rioters who burt government properties and vehicles in Karachi, just as it does in Balochistan?"[73] The MQM is a key ally of the PML-Q in the National Assembly and hence this question of its cadres being given preferential treatment making the federal government guilty of adopting double standards. The killing of Sardar Bugti and the military operations in Balochistan widened the chasm between the military regime and its civilian collaborators, including the PML-Q and MQM. Condemnation against the killing of Sardar Bugti cut across all party lines. The National Assembly reverberated with the slogan, 'Qatil, Qatil, General Qatil', (Killer, Killer, General is Killer). Leaders of the PPPP, PML-N, JWP, Pashtunkhawa Milli Awami Party, Balochistan National Party, and Pakistan Tehrik-e-Insaaf severely criticised the killing and Liaquat Baloch of the MMA called for a united opposition to overthrow the Military from politics. The opposition decided to move a motion against the killing in the National Assembly which was blocked by the Speaker.[74] Although the MMA made several statements in the National Assembly along with the rest of the opposition but it has refrained from taking onto the streets or making a big issue of the crisis. It considered it wise to limit its response to verbal criticism and not come on the streets which may have made its cadre the target of the Military.

Conclusion

The MMA has nurtured its areas of influence particularly in the NWFP and Balochistan and the victory of JI in the Karachi local elections has given the MMA some leverage in Sindh too, provided the conglomeration remains intact and does not fall apart. Observers of Pakistan affairs believe that the MMA is not a temporary phenomenon in politics. Kalim Bahadur, former professor, Jawaharlal Nehru University said, "The MMA is not going to be untouchable anymore. They are here to stay. This will also be helped by the fact that the Military will never like Benazir and Nawaz to stage a comeback in the foreseeable future."[75] Rasul Baksh Rais says, "It is not my argument that MMA is the best candidate for taking Pakistan to the destination of Western Liberalism: quite the opposite. But like any other party, they have constitutional and moral right to compete for political power, and after winning elections, they have right and responsibility to implement their agenda."[76] The MMA has even started chewing into PML-Q's area of influence. The case in point is the victory of MMA over PML-Q, in the January 2003 by-election for the Rawalpindi seat, which has been a stronghold of the PPP and PML-N and is also the headquarters of the Military.[77]

The rise of the MMA surely qualifies as a watershed in Pakistan's wavered democratic history. It has been quick to learn how to secure its interests in a political environment where there are no permanent friends or foes. In spite of its differences with General Musharraf over its Islamisation agenda, it refrained from voting against the PML-Q and managed to remain in power. Having said that it must be mentioned that it also faced substantial loss of credibility due to its role in General Musharraf's political schemes. It antagonised the ARD constituents and caused differences within the MMA as well. The MMA's support to General Musharraf's LFO undermined the struggle for the restoration of democracy in Pakistan. Mounting political pressures on General Musharraf's 'guided democracy' fizzled out due to the MMA's backtracking. Critics said that the party succumbed to its narrow self-interest both at the national and provincial levels, at the expense of democracy. Not surprisingly, the party looked desperate to redeem its lost credibility by distancing itself from General Musharraf.

But the biggest challenge for the MMA is its unity with its strength becoming its weakness, as well. The JUI-(S) had left the MMA in protest over the domineering role of Qazi Hussain Ahmed and the Liaquat Baloch led JI and the Fazl-ur Rehman led JUI-F, in the internal affairs of the MMA, and the party's role in facilitating the passing of the 17th Amendment. Maulana Sajjid Mir's Jamiat-e-Ahle Hadith and Allama Sajjid Naqvi's Pakistan Islami Tehrik also announced their detachment from the conglomeration, making the MMA virtually a two-party (JI and JUI-F) alliance.[78] Therefore, with differences emerging between the JI and JUI-F over the latter's decision to attend the NSC meeting and appointment of Muhammad Khan Sherani—JUI-F's Balochistan unit chief—as chairman of the National Assembly Standing Committee, the future does not auger well for the MMA. The desertion by the other small parties within the MMA would not matter as much as the confrontation between the JI and JUI-F would, given the fact that they are the biggest and the most influential parties in terms of their grassroots support and cadre network. If the JI and JUI-F can stick together, they may make a huge difference in the next general elections. Such a possibility is also shared by General Musharraf who appears determined to defeat his former allies (the MMA) in the next elections. He wrote in his book, *In the Line of Fire* that it has become necessary to defeat the religious alliance in the next elections to bolster his enlightened moderation and clear the domestic mess in Pakistan due to sectarian and ethnic disturbances and the MMA's Islamisation drive. Understandably, in the run-up to the next general elections, both sides are scurrying for a political alliance with the ARD constituent parties. At present, General Musharraf looks inclined to reach an understanding with the PPPP and speculations of a possible deal got stronger with the release of Asif Ali Zardari from jail. In addition, his name was removed from the Exit Control List (ECL). Similarly, Hamza Shahbaz, son of Shahbaz Sharif, has also been removed from the ECL but his chances of reaching any understanding with Nawaz Sharif appear remote. The political vendetta between General Musharraf and Nawaz Sharif stems from the latter's past acts such as scrapping of the Article 58 (2) b, unceremonious sacking of General Musharraf in absentia, denial of permission for his plane to land on the way back from Sri Lanka, and an incessant barrage of statements against him while in exile. There are reports of parleys between General Musharraf and the PPPP which may materialise into a mutually beneficial political deal before the elections. The MMA's efforts at burying the hatchet with the ARD have been scuttled largely due to their past links with the Military regime and their role in facilitating General Musharraf's range of anti-democratic measures. In December 2006, the MMA was very upset with the amendment in the Hudood Ordinance and stepped up its opposition against General Musharraf. This political confrontation is only going to intensify in the future, wherein the Islamist parties and the Jihadi groups may join hands against General Musharraf's regime who is also seen as an agent of US policy towards Pakistan. How critical is the power and influence of the Jihadis in Pakistan's future stability and security? How deep and serious are their links in the establishment? These are some very pertinent questions which deserve some serious attention. The next chapter unravels the Military's and the Inter-Services Intelligence's (ISI) relationship with the Jihadis in Pakistan and how it created a Frankenstein monster, which now threatens security and stability of Pakistan and challenges the entire State apparatus itself.

NOTES

1. Raja Asghar, "NA Prorogued Amid Protests: No Business on Third Day" at http://www.dawn.com/2002/03/11/nat.htmMarch 11, 2003.
2. "State of Democracy Report, Revival of Democracy-1st year of Democracy", November 16, 2002-November 15, 2003, Pakistan Institute for Legislative Development and Transparency (PILDAT), p. 1.
3. "State of Democracy Report", November 16, 2003-March 31, 2004, Pakistan Institute for Legislative Development and Transparency (PILDAT), p. 8.
4. Ahmed Hasan, "MMA, Govt. Sign Deal: Govt. Sacking to be

Referred to SC, NSC Formation Through Parliament, No Extension in Superior Court Judges' Retirement Age" at http://www.dawn.com/2003/12/25/top2.htm

5. Currently six constitutional petitions lay pending in the Supreme Court challenging the legality and legitimacy of the 17th amendment. See "Govt. Submits Reply in Pleas Against 17th Amendment" at http://www.dawn.com/2005/03/28/nat1.htm
6. "State of Democracy Report", November 16, 2003-November 31, 2004, Pakistan Institute for Legislative Development and Transparency (PILDAT), p. 1.
7. "Opp. MPs Slam Govt.-MMA Deal" at http://www.dailytimes.com.pk/default.asp?page=story>28-12-2003_pg7_27
8. "State of Democracy Report", no. 3, p. 9. Also see Ahmed Hasan, no. 4.
9. "MMA Supported 17th Amendment to Save System: Hafiz", at http://www.paktribune.com/news/index.php?id=83223
10. "MMA Denies Deal, Rules Out Acceptance of Ministerial Berths" at http://paktribune.com/news/index.php?id=49975
11. "State of Democracy Report", April 1, 2004-June 30, 2004, Pakistan Institute for Legislative Development and Transparency (PILDAT), p. 2.
12. The PPPP had secured 81 seats in the NA in the 2002 elections, but later 21 PPP-P members had defected after taking oath, with 18 of them forming the PPP-Patriots and three joining the PML-Q. One PPP-P member from Rahim Yar Khan, Zafar Iqbal Warraich, also quit the party and resigned from his seat in the National Assembly, but later won the same seat in the by-election on a PML-Q ticket and returned to the National Assembly. Besides the PPP-P also lost in the by-election one of the two seats won by Chaudhry Aitzaz Ahsan. Like the PPP-P, the MMA supporters also defected, as seven of the 12 members from the Federally Administered Tribal Areas (FATA) parted ways, reducing the MMA's strength from 68 seats to 60 seats. Ironically, the NA Speaker accepted the MMA's claim of 68 seats and rejected the PPP-P's claim, despite the fact that it had the support of other Opposition groups as well.
13. Raja Ashgar, "General Musharraf Wins Vote of Confidence", at http://www.dawn.com/2004/01/02/top1.htm

14. Ibid.
15. Hasan Askari Rizvi, "Musharraf's Army Uniform", at http://www.dailytimes.com.pk/default.asp?page=story_13-9-2004_pg3_2
16. Ahmed Hasan and Amir Wasim, "Cabinet Wants Musharraf to Keep Both Posts; President will Agree, Hopes Rashid", at http://www.dawn.com/2004/09/16/top1.htm
17. Ibid.
18. Mubasher Bukhari, "PA Resolution demands Musharraf keep Uniform", at http://www.dailytimes.com.pk/print.asp?page=story_14-9-2004_pg1_3&ndate=09/16/2004%201:16:48%20PM
19. Mohammed Riaz, "Musharraf Should Quit One Office: Frontier PA", at http://www.dawn.com/2004/09/16/top3.htm
20. "Treasury Withdraws Resolution in Favour of Musharraf Uniform in BA", at http://www.paktribune.com/news/
21. Shamim-ur-Rehman, "Sindh PA Supports President in Uniform", at http://www.dawn.com/2004/09/03/top3.htm
22. Raja Asghar and Ahmed Hassan, "Dual Office Bill Passed Amid Protests", at http://www.dawn.com/2004/10/15/top4.htm
23. Raja Asghar, "Senate Passes Twin-Office Bill Amid Protests", at http://www.dawn.com/2004/11/02/top1.htm
24. "Opposition Cries Foul on Rashid's Remarks: Musharraf's Army's Post", at http://www.dawn.com/2004/09/16/top2.htm
25. Ibid.
26. Raja Asghar, "NA Adopts NSC Bill Amid Uproar: MQM Amendments Incorporated" at http://www.dawn.com/2004/04/08/top1.htm
27. Raja Asghar, "Opposition Cries Foul As NSC Bill is Passed", at http://www.dawn.com/2004/04/15/top1.htm
28. Ibid.
29. Ibid.
30. "State of Democracy Report", April 1, 2004-June 30, 2004, Pakistan Institute for Legislative Development and Transparency (PILDAT), p. 8.
31. Raja Asghar, no. 19. Interestingly, in the original bill the functions of the NSC included "matters relating to democracy, governance, and inter-provincial harmony", which was replaced later with

"crisis management". The government must have realised that earlier terminology may raise serious concerns over the purpose of the NSC.

32. Ibid.
33. Ibid.
34. "JUI-F Calls for End to NSC Boycott" at http://www.dawn.com/2005/03/07/top4.htm
35. Qamar Jabbar, "MMA Divided Over Attending NSC Meeting", at http://www.dailytimes.com.pk/default.asp?page=story_16-2-2005_pg7_14
36. Ismail Khan, "JUI-F Approach to the NSC", at http://www.http://www.dawn.com/2005/03/09/top4.htm
37. Zakir Hassnain, "Akram Durrani Speaks in NWFP Assembly: '29,360 dead, 7,000 missing, Rs 32b loss', at http://www.dailytimes.com.pk/default.asp?page=2005%5C11%5C16%5Cstory_16-11-2005_pg7_30
38. Ibid.
39. "State of Democracy Report", April 1, 2004-June 30, 2004, Pakistan Institute for Legislative Development and Transparency (PILDAT), p. 9.
40. Ibid, p. 10.
41. Akhtar Amin, "14 Peshawar UC Nazims Resign in Protest", at http://www.jang-group.com/thenews/may2004-daily/05-05-2004/national/n4.htm
42. Iqbal Khattak, "MMA Impending District Governments in NWFP", at http://www.dailytimes.com.pk/default.asp?page=story_9-1-2003_pg7_26
43. "State of Democracy Report", no. 3, p. 10.
44. "General Musharraf Appoints Khalilur Rehman as New Governor NWFP", at http://pakistantimes.net/2005/03/13/top3.htm
45. Zulfiqar Ali, "Fazl Accuses General Musharraf of Supporting PPP", at http://www.dawn.com/2005/03/29/top2.htm
46. "MMA March: Durrani Vetoes Nazim's Order", at http://www.dawn.com/2005/03/28/nat7.htm
47. Iqbal Khattak, no. 42.
48. Mazhar Abbas, "Why MQM Wants JI Banned?" *Friday Times*, July 23-29, 2004, p. 5.
49. "Constitutional Status", at http://www.geocities.com/fataonline/

constitutional.htm

50. See Appendix I.
51. Muhhammad Shehzad, "General Musharraf's Biggest Quandry: The On-going Waziristan Resistance", at http://www.satribune.com/archives/nov04/P1_msh.htm
52. Rahimullah Yusufzai, "Analysis: Pakistan's Army In the Tribal Areas", at http://www.news.bbc.co.uk/1/low/world/south_asia/3020552.stm
53. "MMA Legislators Infuriated Over Wana Operations" at http://www.jang.com.pk/the news/mar2004-daily/18-03-2004/metro/k4.htm
54. The Pakistan government claims that there are Uzbek, Chechen and Arab militants operating in the areas. See Muhammad Najeeb, "Pakistan Opposition Questions Anti-terror Raid" at http://www.southasiamonotor.org/pak/2004/sept/10pak2.shtml
55. Shehzada Raza, "No Let-up in Tribal Offensive, Says Faisal", at http://www.dailytimes.com.pk/default.asp?page=story_19-3-2004_pg7_26
56. "MMA Rejects Wana Operations", at http://www.dailytimes.com.pk/default.asp?page=story_11-1-2004-pg7_37
57. Ibid.
58. "Foreigners Registration", *The News*, July 8, 2004, at http://www.infopak.gov.pk/writeups/foreigner's_reg.htm
59. Mubashir Zaidi, "State of Confusion", *Herald*, February 2005, p. 64.
60. Syed Shoib Hasan, "Battle Front Sui", *Herald*, February 2005, pp. 54-58.
61. Ibid.
62. "Bugti Rejects Balochistan Committee's Recommendations, Aziz Assures Implementation of Balochistan Committee's Recommendations", March 22, 2005 at http://www.paktribune.com/news/index.php?id=98757
63. Ibid.
64. Azizullah Khan, "Wining to Lose," *Herald*, February 2005, p. 65.
65. "Reality Check", *Herald*, February 2005, p. 14.
66. "Government to Ensure Implementation of Recommendations of Parliamentary Committee on Balochistan: President", Press

Release at http://presidentofpakistan.gov.pk/PRPressRelease

67. "MMA Criticizes Plan for New Cantonments", at http://www.dawn.com/2005/02/23/nat9.htm
68. Mubashir Zaidi, no. 59, p. 65.
69. Saleem Shahid, "Bugti Killed in Operation: Six Officers among 21 Security Personnel Dead", at http://www.dawn.com/2006/08/27/top1.htm
70. Ibid.
71. "Writ at all Costs: Musharraf", at http://www.dawn.com/2006/08/28/top2.htm
72. Massoud Ansari, "The Battle for Balochistan", *Newsline*, September 2006, p. 23.
73. "When Mobs in Karachi Burn down Public Property, is Military Action taken against Them-Jamal?-Jamali Bugti" *Newsline*, September 2006, p. 32.
74. Raja Ashgar, "Opposition's NA Session on Bugti", at http://www.dawn.com/2006/08/29/top5.htm
75. Interview with the author, New Delhi. February 2, 2003.
76. Rasul Baksh Rais, "Rise of Religious Parties", *The News,* October 19, 2002 at www.jang.com.pk/thenews/oct2002-daily/19-10-2002/oped/opinion.htm
77. Raja Asghar, "PML-Q, MMA Win Majority Seats" at http://www.dawn.com/2003/01/17/top1.htm
78. Alya Alvi, "The Never Ending Split in MMA", at http://pakistantimes.net/2005/07/05/oped3.htm

CHAPTERV

Military and the Jihadis
Friends Turned Foes?

This chapter looks into the Military's relationship with Jihadi groups in Pakistan and the extent to which Jihadi ideals have penetrated into the top, middle and lower strata of the Military. It investigates the Military-Jihadi-ISI triangular liaisons in various cases that have had far-reaching consequences for Pakistan and international security. Cracks have emerged in this triangular relationship, primarily following Pakistan's participation in the global war against terrorism and drive against domestic Jihadi outfits, triggering a spate of assassination bids on General Musharraf and other military officers. This chapter also analyses the sources of these assassination attempts and assesses their long-term implications for Pakistan's internal security.

Until two years back, if one accessed the website of the Pakistani military, a loud roar of *Nara-e-Takbeer— Allah O Akbar* greeted the surfers on the homepage. No other ministry or institutional website had such a feature. This feature seemed deliberate, for it sought to achieve twin purposes. One, it projected the Military as the sole upholder and protector of Islam and two, it in a way accorded religious legitimacy for its role and rule in Pakistan. Islam and jihad have always formed the nucleus of Pakistani Military's working at the domestic as well as international levels. The use of Islam and Jihadis by the army since 1970 has come to challenge the writ of this very institution today.

Back in history, one finds that the preliminary boost to the role of mullahs, mystics, *madaris* and mosques in governance and politics came when the First Constituent Assembly in order to consolidate and expand its power base through religion, sought to appropriate Islamic terminology and its ideological metaphors in State affairs.[1] In 1956, the first Constitution containing 234 Articles was passed, making Pakistan an Islamic State.[2] After the initial quandary during Field Marshal Ayub Khan's tenure over the role of Islam in politics[3], the title 'Islamic' in was withdrawn by him in 1962, and then reinstated in 1963, under protest from the Ulema. According to I.A. Rehman, "Even Ayub Khan, considered in many quarters as a secular commander, fell back on the religious slogan when the 1965 conflict with India began. The literature and music related to the conflicts the Pakistan army has faced are saturated with religiosity".[4] This encouraged the mullahs in Pakistan who were already on the Islamisation path, agitating against the Ahmediyas and pressurising the military regime to declare them as non-Muslims.

A formal endeavour, *per se,* to structure ties with the Islamists was made under General Yahya Khan in 1970 to counter the opposition in the form of Zulfiqar Ali Bhutto's Pakistan Peoples' Party in West Pakistan and Bengali nationalists led by Sheikh Mujibur Rehman in East Pakistan. With the army's support the religious parties even won 18 out of 300 seats in the National Assembly in the 1970 elections. The army remained in cahoots with the Islamists against Zulfiqar Ali Bhutto and soon drifted into an Islamisation drive under General Zia when Soviet Union invaded Afghanistan in 1979. *Madaris* mushroomed and *Mujahideen* including Gulbuddin Hekmatyar and Burhanuddin Rabbani began to spearhead Pakistan's resistance to the Soviet forces in Afghanistan. Towards the mid-1990s the Taliban came into being and in Pakistan conservatism had begun to take deep roots in the army ranks, and army units and cantonments began to organise regular sermons by clerics including Mufti Saeed and Sufi Iqbal and Tablighi Jamaat members. The official cadres in the army began to show sign of conservatism and the earlier practice to seek permission to grow a beard in the armed forces was also abolished by General Zia in 1976. I.A. Rehman finds four distinct measures taken under his rule which not only cemented the Military-Ulema relationship further but also enhanced the influence of Islam and conservative clerics in the Military. These were:

- *First*, providing generous facilities for religious seminaries while restricting the growth of traditional educational institutions;
- *second*, allowing the clerics to join the legislatures, the bureaucracy and the judiciary;
- *third*, projecting the armed forces as the saviour of Pakistan's ideological frontiers; and
- *fourth*, making promotion to senior ranks in the armed forces based on one's demonstration of qualities the Chief Martial Law Administrator considered essential in a holy warrior. The result was a large section in the armed forces becoming staunch supporters of the Talibanisation of Pakistan.[5]

Over the years a large number of *madaris*, sectarian and political parties and Jihadi groups have proliferated, having close links with the establishment. It is this comprehensive network of Jihadis sustained with the army's and ISI's support which has become a serious challenge for General Musharraf today. The Genie is out of the bottle!

Islam-Military Linkage Rationale: Professional or Ideological?

It is no secret that the Islamisation of the Pakistan Army gained vigour and speed under General Zia to deal with the situation in neighbouring Afghanistan. He provided the army with the motto of *Iman* (Faith), *Taqwa* (piety) and *Jihad e-Sibilliliah* (struggle in the service of Allah!). The army got a crusading image and projected Pakistan as an invincible fortress of Islam between Allah-in-his-heaven and Army-on-earth. Zia donned the mantle of a m*ujahid* (holy warrior) who would enforce ancient glory of Islamic *Ummah*. He invoked the magic word of 'Islam' to mesmerise his supporters, disarm his detractors and silence his critics. However, the adverse impact this approach had on the army high command was the tension it created between the 'modern westernised professionals' and the '*mujahideen*'. The professional image of the force fast began to wane.[6]

According to Brian Cloughley, "He (Zia) discouraged the teaching of English. He encouraged rote-learning of religious detail at the expense of improvement in intellectual probity...his regime and the years thereafter spawned a large number of blinkered, semi-educated youngsters whose expectations are greater than their competence to realize them... Some below-standard young men join the army as officer cadets". [7]

There is very limited study or record of the officers who were commissioned during General Zia's 'Islamic' regime. It would be interesting to analyse their orientation and inclination in their official working. Stephen Cohen, by far the closest to exploring this aspect provides an interesting perspective on this in his book '*The Idea of Pakistan*'. He argues that the officers who came into the army during Zia's tenure and have now reached the rank of Major or Colonel, are definitely more conservative than their predecessors. Some were also noticed in Afghanistan supporting Taliban fighters, in direct contradiction of the official policy.[8] He explains further:

> *Drawn increasingly from rural Pakistan or from smaller towns and cities, such officers often begin with a distorted image of the West, reflecting the deepening anti-West sentiments prevalent in the country. Pakistani officers have come to believe that the West has targeted the Islamic world and Pakistan in particular. Like many Islamists they think Muslims are subjected to discrimination and army oppression throughout the world—in Palestine, Bosnia, the Philippines, Iraq, and Chechnya—simply because they are Muslims. The more simplistic ones assume a "Zionist"-American alliance, and despite their favourable view of the United States as land of opportunity, many believe that Washington favours Hindu India and thus is no longer an ally, but a strategic threat to Pakistan.*
>
> *These beliefs are deeply entrenched in the officer corps, and changing them will require extended contacts with the*

> *West and a more liberal social and educational environment. If the Pakistan army does move further down the road of Islamic parochialism, one reason will be that it was cut off from those Western contacts that had been a liberalizing force for its first 30 years. In a sentence, younger officers reflect the larger society, and to this extent they are becoming more "Islamic" and anti-West.*[9]

Under Zia, the officer corps was seen to be more "Islamic" than it was thirty or forty years ago, and more openly supportive of Islamic forces and groups. Nineteen retired Generals attended the 1991 convention of the Jamaat-e-Islami in Islamabad and there are strong links between the army, various Islamist groups and retired ISI officers who are still working with their former "clients".[10] The influence of the sunni organization, the Tablighi Jamaat (TJ) has grown in influence in the officer corps as its social base and influence increased in Pakistan. This group was allowed to enter armed forces' premises by General Zia for purely preaching purposes.[11]

Ahmed Rashid, a noted journalist and author of *Taliban*, said in an interview:

> *There is a great degree [more] of Islamisation in the army than what you had before because so many officers have been involved in Afghanistan and Kashmir and there has been a radicalization of the army. After 9/11, a long-term programme was needed to reassess the education of army officers. That has not happened so far. What exists are a lot of middle-level officers who were inducted during the 1980s at the height of the Afghanistan jihad. Many of them were inducted from the religious schools. They became more radical during the 1990s in the Afghan and the Kashmir war. These officers are also looking at the corruption of the generals, the perks and privileges, the plots, houses, etc. where Musharraf is just buying them off... there would be resentment on that front too. Certainly they will form a critical element against what Musharraf's policies are right now.*[12]

Owen Bennett Jones has provided a very interesting analysis of the mullah-army interface in his book *Pakistan: Eye of the Storm,* which says that army's getting closer to the Jihadis for operations across the borders has led to the radicalisation of the forces to a large extent. Quoting an officer, he says that only 3 per cent of the army could be described as extremists, if 5 per cent of the Pakistan's population is considered extremists. At the top there are only a small percentage of officers with strong religious views. However, Jones makes a key point when he says that the army may face a split in the face of an Islamic revolution and a common soldier may refuse to fire on the civilians in such a scenario, which suggests the tenor of Islam in the army—though currently—very nascent may transform into radicalisation, if triggered through a mass upheaval. He remarks, "Those in the army who favour Islamic revolution may be in the minority but that may not matter. If it were ever faced with mass Islam-inspired street protests in Pakistan, the army leadership could find itself facing an awkward dilemma. An order to fire on such a crowd could well be disobeyed by some of the men. Such an outcome, creating conditions in which the army might be split, would be viewed as catastrophic by the army which has always considered the maintenance of unity as being one of its highest priorities."[13]

Over the years, some senior Generals have been known for their hardline Islamic approach and fundamentalist thinking. The likes of Lieutenant General Muhammad Aziz Khan are recognized as "fundamentalist" by Stephen Cohen too[14]. The others who can be identified as "fundamentalist" to a large extent include Lieutenant General(s) Mehmud Ahmed, Muzaffar Usmani (the two other players in General Musharraf's 1999 coup), and Hamid Gul.

General Muhammad Aziz Khan

After the coup, it was General Aziz who called the shots while General Musharraf ran the regime. All appointments had to be approved by him and every minister and senior government official had to go through the 'Aziz channel'. He also had a serious bearing on Pakistan's policy towards Kashmir, the Comprehensive Test Ban Treaty (CTBT) and Afghanistan. On the CTBT issue particularly, there were sharp differences between Aziz and Musharraf with the former against the latter's view of signing the Treaty. General Aziz and like-minded "Jihadi" generals exerted total control over Islamic militancy in Kashmir and relations with the Taliban regime. Over the years, Jamaat-e-Islami is reported to have established strong links with the "jihadi" generals.[15]

An exception was made for General Aziz, when owing to his hardline views and influence on the jihadi elements in Pakistan, he was elevated to the rank of Lieutenant General without ever having commanded a corps. A key player in Musharraf's Kargil misadventure, Aziz as a Brigadier and deputy army secretary to Zia-ul Haq was known for his hardline Islamic thinking, passion for the Kashmir insurgency (himself being a Kashmiri of the Sudan tribe) and liking for the Taliban.[16]

Before he retired, he was Chairman, Joint Chiefs of Staff (CJCS), a position to which he was elevated by Musharraf, perhaps against the former's liking so as to neutralise his aspirations and contention for the Army Chief's post. General Aziz, along with Muzaffar Usmani, was seen packing before the December 31, 2004 uniform deadline dangling over Musharraf. Experts say Musharraf did not want the army to have ambitious, powerful and fundamentalist officers who could have exploited any unexpected development as the December 31 deadline approached.[17] Even after General Aziz retired, Musharraf has been keenly watching his movements with regard to the Kashmiri Jihadi groups and the Taliban. Aziz is a popular figure among the lower ranks of the army and hails from the village of some of the conspirators of Musharraf's failed assassination attempt. It is also believed that Musharraf, by seeking his extension, blocked General Aziz's chances to be the Army Chief much to the dislike of the latter's tribe in POK. [18]

Lieutenant General Mehmud Ahmed

Lieutenant General Mehmud Ahmed, was Corps Commander Rawalpindi, when the coup was staged in October 1999. He was the Director-General Inter-Services Intelligence (DG-ISI) and following the September 11 attacks, he was removed from this coveted post by General Musharraf at the United States' behest. The US' Federal Bureau of Investigation (FBI) team had unearthed credible links between him and Omar Sheikh, a key conspirator in the Daniel Pearl murder case and arranger of finances for the September 11 attacks. It is believed that it was at General Mehmud's instruction that Shiekh had transferred $1,00,000 into the account of Mohammad Atta, one of the lead terrorists involved in the attacks.[19] Interestingly, the morning of September 11, General Mehmud was meeting Deputy Secretary Richard Armitage, and Central Intelligence Agency (CIA) Director George Tenet in Washington.[20] Another meeting was held between Senator Bob Graham and Porter Gross with Maleeha Lodhi, the Pakistani Ambassador to the US, and Mehmud Khan. The agenda was a follow up action to the visit of the Senators' trip to Pakistan to discuss the prospects of the extradition of Osama bin Laden with General Musharraf. Reports say that Musharraf had expressed his helplessness in the matter calling it a bilateral issue between Washington and Kabul.[21] In the meetings, Mehmud Khan is said to have spoken very highly of the Taliban leader Mullah Omar, calling him a 'religious and non violent man with humanitarian instincts' who had to 'suffer greatly' at the hands of Afghan warlords.[22]

The most infamous act of General Mehmud is considered to be his trip to Kandahar on September 17, 2001, after the WTC attacks, at the insistence of General Musharraf to persuade Mullah Omar to hand over Osama bin Laden to the US. Mehmud Khan instead advised the Taliban supremo to resist and stand up against the building US threat. Someone in the delegation spilled the beans and General Mehmud was replaced by Lieutenant General Ehsan ul Haq as the ISI chief.[23]

Lieutenant General Hamid Gul

Considered a hawk and hardline Islamist, Lieutenant General Hamid Gul, also the former ISI chief, held that Islam was the ideology and jihad was its instrument. A Jamaat member, Gul's hardline Islamic backs the need for Pakistan to Islamise itself to ward off superpowers' pressure so as to be of some match to India, were also shared by his Army Chief, General Mirza Aslam Beg. Hamid Gul along with General Javed Nasir was known to be having strong links with the Jamaat.

Originally, a trusted American ally against the Soviets, General Gul's resentment against the West and the US began to germinate when the US launched the war against the Taliban, which according to him was a huge 'betrayal'. Even now, he serves as an advisor to the religious parties in Pakistan and contends that the September 11 attacks were carried out by Mossad and its US accomplices and not by Osama bin Laden. He accepts that the chain of events since September 11 have made him more fundamentalist than he was during the war against the Soviets. He has high regards for the Taliban. In appreciation, he says, "They represent Islam in its purest form so far. It's a clean sheet. And they were also moving in the right direction when this crisis was cooked up the by the US. Until September 11, they had perfect law and order with no formal police force, only traffic cops without sidearms. Now, in less than two weeks, they have mobilized some 3,00,000 volunteers to fight American and British invaders if they come". [24]

Hand in Glove: Army/ISI-Jihadi Relations

After decades of working with the Jihadis, a forced turnaround in Pakistan's policies came as a severe jolt to the Jihadi groups and its promoters both within and outside the army and ISI. It was a testing time and not easy to cope with both the army and the Jihadis. Muhammad Amir Rana comments, "As the modern Jihadi culture was created, nurtured and groomed in Pakistan, its effect on the many senior people involved in that process, coupled with the massive public support which was state sponsored, should not be underestimated. The psychological trauma involved in changing sides cannot easily be washed off…The Jihadis have many supporters in the Pakistan army and secret services. It is extremely unlikely that none of them would be 'helping out' their former friends and allies".[25]

There are a large number of cases wherein the convergence of interests between the Jihadis and their army and ISI masters could be traced at the level of a sectarian feud within Pakistan, nuclear proliferation, drug trafficking and Jihad in Afghanistan and Kashmir. Of these the following solicit attention.

JKLF-ISI Linkage

In June 2005, the Jammu and Kashmir Liberation Front (JKLF)[26] Chairman Yasin Malik said, "Sheikh Ahmed Rashid had played a great role for the Kashmir's liberation. He used to support the frontline jihadis from Kashmir, but few know of his contribution".[27] The statement made to compliment Sheikh Rashid exposed the skeletons in the 'jihadi' cupboard, creating a furore more in India than in Pakistan. What followed was a spate of denials and clarifications from both Malik and Rashid, but the damage had been done. The support of ISI and the Pakistani State to militancy in Kashmir is no secret, but whenever such an exposé is made, it puts Pakistan foreign office in a quandary. In fact, intelligence sources confirm that Rashid had rented his farmhouse to the ISI which was being used by the agency for harbouring militants that Malik referred to. Apart from Malik, the POK JKLF Chief Amanuallah Khan also claimed' "We had a gentleman's agreement, an oral sort of agreement. I was given assurances that the ISI was all out for the independence of Jammu and Kashmir".[28] Also, a Pakistan People's Party spokesperson said that the Freedom House in Rawalpindi was a militant training camp and in 1989 the ISI had been given vast tracts of land without the government's permission for the purpose.[29]

Army-ISI-Taliban Linkage

It is said that following September 11 attacks, a clandestine visit by ISI operatives to Kandahar, in defiance of General Musharraf's orders, to help the Taliban build the defences, had brought US-Pakistan relations on collision course. Ahmed Rashid told *The Times of India,* "Senior retired army officers said that General Musharraf was infuriated when informed of the officers' trip because it could have jeopardized Pakistan's relations with the United States and Britain. There is no suggestion that General (Mehmud) Ahmed knew about the trip either, but he nevertheless resigned as ISI chief."[30]

There have been several reports which exposed the understanding and linkage between the army and Taliban. The Indian intelligence agencies have been tipping off the Americans that army goods, including ammunition and fuel, were being sent with the help of conduits in the Pakistani government. It was said that the goods travelled from Quetta to Pakistan's border town of Chaman and then on to Kandahar, the Taliban stronghold. All this was done after sunset when official monitoring of the border used to cease for the day.[31]

Pakistan Army's relations with the Taliban and several Jihadi groups have been a matter of concern for the US and had featured in the conversation between George Bush and Pervez Musharraf repeatedly. According to the Pattern of Global Terrorism 2000, Harkat-ul-Mujahideen and Lashkar-e-Toiba now known as Jamaat-ud-Dawa were specifically mentioned in this regard. Though the Pakistani authorities have denied the charges in the report, intelligence sources pointed to close ties between senior members of Pakistan's Army and ISI with the two groups. There have also been serious allegations that Pakistan's ISI has active links with both the Taliban regime's intelligence service and Osama bin Laden himself. As per local intelligence sources, the Pakistani authorities have provided medical facilities for the ailing Bin Laden, including renal dialysis, at an army hospital in Peshawar. It is believed that without any logistical and other kind of support from Islamabad, the Taliban would not have continued to function the way it has been functioning.[32]

Army-Taliban: Kunduz Evacuation

Another instance of army-Jihadi convergence was the airlift in Kunduz, Afghanistan carried out by the Pakistani Air Force in the middle of the war. In November 2001, when the coalition forces along with the Northern Alliance began to squeeze the Taliban and Al Qaida fighters in the northern hill town of Kunduz, the Pakistani government developed cold feet. The reason—along with the trapped Taliban fighters there were Pakistani Army officers, intelligence advisers, and volunteers who were fighting alongside the Taliban.

Subsequent reports showed that Pakistani airplanes carried the airlift and General Musharraf sought George W. Bush's permission for the evacuation on the pretext that these officers were fighting for the coalition forces and their loss or capture would create a domestic stir in Pakistan. The permission was granted, but the US officials admitted that the operations undertaken in C-130 planes were thought to be of a limited nature, which finally evacuated around 1,000 pro-Taliban fighters, as it got out of hand. The Pakistani troops fighting for the Taliban were evacuated, and along with them Taliban and Al-Qaida cadres also escaped to Pakistan. CIA officials also believed that several Taliban leaders were amongst the evacuees.[33]

Ahmed al-Khadir Episode: ISI's Role

In yet another instance, the ISI and the army in collusion with the Taliban helped an Egyptian associate of Osama bin Laden, known as Ahmed al-Khadir escape to Afghanistan. Tim McGirk says that Ahmed al-Khadir was wanted in the connection with the bombings of the Egyptian Embassy in Islamabad in 1995 in which 15 people had died. The Egyptian having known of Ahmed's presence in a safe house in Peshawar, surrounded the house and informed the ISI Chief General Mehmud Ahmed. This turned out to be a blunder on the part of the Egyptians. No security force came and instead a car with diplomatic license plate and Taliban officials arrived and frisked Al-Khadir to Afghanistan via the Khyber Pass. Later, the official explanation said, "So sorry. The man gave us the slip".[34] Ahmed Rashid says that safe houses were used by the Al-Qaida agents as they came into Pakistan from Afghanistan. The ISI has been constantly training new recruits for Jihadi activities and also laundering money for the terrorist activities through the global *hawala* network, which explains the fiasco, says Rashid. In the same vein, Osama bin Laden was also allowed to slip away when an operation undertaken by a US-trained Pakistani commando unit under ISI supervision did not do the "squat".[35]

Omar Saeed Sheikh and Daniel Pearl Kidnapping

Omar Saeed Sheikh was the brain behind the kidnapping of three

Britons and an American in Kashmir in 1994. The victims were subsequently rescued by the Indian security forces and Saeed Sheikh was apprehended. In a turn of events, Saeed Sheikh was released along with Masood Azhar (founder of Jaish-e Muhammad) as trade-off for the lives of passengers aboard the Indian Airlines flight IC-814 that was hijacked in December 2001 by his group named the National Youth Movement for the Sovereignty of Pakistan. In February 2002, Sheikh kidnapped another Westerner in Daniel Pearl, a Wall Street journalist. Though Sheikh was sentenced to death by the Terrorism Court on July 15, 2002, yet he is still alive and confined to the secured walls of the Hyderabad Jail. The high security around him remains as authorities fear that his cohorts may try to rescue him.[36]

The events surrounding him are as controversial as the man himself. After the December 13, 2001 Indian Parliament attack, in which the involvement of Sheikh has also been established, a livid Musharraf is said to have barged into the ISI headquarters screaming at the ISI Director General (Internal Security), "Leash in these mad dogs that you have kept".[37] In the Daniel Pearl episode, Pervez Musharraf in February 2002 had remarked blatantly that Daniel Pearl was a victim of "intelligence games" and was "over inquisitive" and "getting involved" in the story (Pearl was in Pakistan in connection with an investigative story he was doing on Richard Reid, the shoe bomber at WTC).[38] These were evidence that the establishment including the top army leadership in Pakistan was uncomfortable with what Daniel Pearl was investigating. Plus, the demands which the kidnappers put forward as a price for the release of Daniel Pearl included supply of F-16 fighters to Pakistan. It is beyond imagination to think that Omar Sheikh's group wanted these fighters to boost their profile or to augment their terrorist operations against India or the US forces in Afghanistan. The intended recipient was obviously the Pakistan Army, which till date is waiting for the fighters. It is reported that when Omar Sheikh was put under pressure by the army and ISI to surrender, he struck a deal that he would only surrender before the person of his choice and he would not be extradited to the US. Any non-compliance would force him to expose the linkage of the establishment in the case. The Pakistani government agreed and Sheikh surrendered before Brigadier (Retd.) Ijaz Shah, an old ISI official contact of Sheikh, and the then Home Secretary of Punjab (Pakistan).[39]

The Recoil Effect: Army-Jihadis Connivance

With the September 11 attacks, overthrow of the Taliban regime, and the initiation of the peace process in 2003, Musharraf came under intense international pressure to prevail on the Jihadis operating from Pakistan. While negating any official sponsorship of the Jihadis, he nevertheless waged down a crackdown on the militant groups in Pakistan. It created huge resentment in Pakistan more so among the religious parties and senior officials within the army, both retired and serving. Musharraf became the centre of Jihadis' ire who now derived strength from the religions parties, the Taliban and Al-*Qaida* leadership and sympathisers in the army and ISI. Musharraf became the prime target.

On March 23, 2002, Jihadis planned to eliminate Musharraf by storming the Pakistan Day celebrations in Islamabad's parade area with AK-47 assault rifles and grenades. Fortunately for Musharraf, the parade was cancelled due to Muharram and the plan had to be shelved. Again on December 6, 2002, two suicide bombers plotted to kill Musharraf on Eid prayer at the Shah Faisal Mosque in Islamabad, but aborted the plan eventually due to tight security. On March 23, 2003, four missiles were to be fired from the Margalla hills in Islamabad during the Pakistan Day parade, but this time again the parade was cancelled after a tip-off about the attack was received. A month later, on April 26, 2003 an attempt was made to ram an explosive laden truck into Musharraf's convoy. The attack did not materialise as planned and Musharraf escaped Ground zero at Shahrah-e-Faisal, close to the Karachi Airport, due to the jammers deployed on the security vehicles. After a few months, again another similar attempt was made on the Jhanda Chinchi bridge near the 10-Corps headquarters in Rawalpindi. An estimated 250 kilograms of explosive was to be exploded though a remote control device to kill Musharraf, but for the failure of the jammers again. On December 25, 2003, again three suicide bombers tried to dash an explosive-laden vehicle into Musharraf's car, but the General was lucky once more. He survived but the attack killed 14 people including the suicide bombers.

The Jihadis also tried to kill Prime Minister-elect Shaukat Aziz while he was campaigning in Attock on July 30, 2004, and Karachi Corps Commander Lieutenant General Ahsen Saleem Hayat, the present Vice-Chief of Army Staff, in Karachi on June 10, 2004. Shaukat Aziz was targeted for being Musharraf's man who was chosen due to his contacts with the international financial institutions to resurrect Pakistan's economy. And, Ahsen Saleem Hayat was targeted because he was considered a close confidante of Musharraf and also of the US. He is said to have played a sheet-anchor role in Musharraf's anti-terror drive.

As per the initial press reports the assassination attempts on Musharraf were acts of "some misguided Islamic warriors and a bunch of low ranking army and air force personnel" and later the authorities suspected that the December 25 attack was planned by Omar Sheikh, and possibly Abu Faraz al-Libbi, a Libyan Al-Qaida operative, arrested in Mardan on May 4, 2005.[40] The authorities believed that Al-Libbi was reactivating the Al-Qaida network and operations in Pakistan to eliminate the top leadership. Amjad Hussian Farooqui, another Al-Qaida operative responsible for training Jihadis in camps in POK and Afghanistan was allegedly behind the attack on Shaukat Aziz and US Consulate on July 14, 2002.[41]

A sense of urgency is discernible in dealing with the growth of Jihadis within the armed forces. As per reports, over 30 officers of the Pakistan Army and the Pakistan Air Force were detained in the Attock Fort, while 20 are facing court martial proceedings at the Kharian and Pannu Aqil Army Cantonments for their involvement in the assassination attempts on General Musharraf. The chink in the armour was exposed in August 2003 in the wake of arrest of some army officers under the Army Act of 1952 having links with Al-Qaida's chief operative Khalid Sheikh Muhammad, arrested on March 15, 2003 from Rawalpindi. Those arrested for links with Al-Qaida included two army colonels, Abdul Khalid Abbasi belonging to General Headquarters and Abdul Ghaffar of the Army Aviation Command, three Majors, Adil Qudoos, Rohail Faraz and Muhammad

Ataullah and one Captain, Usman Zafar of Mujahid Battalion. In September 2005, the army court sentenced Major Qudoos to 10 years, Colonel Ghaffar to three months and Colonel Abbasi to six months of imprisonment, and the services of Major Ataullah, Major Faraz and Captain Zafar were terminated. Earlier, Mohammad Abdul Islam Siddiqi (Army No. 8831068) of the Defence Services Guard Company of the Punjab Regiment was executed on charges of plotting to kill Musharraf in the Jhanda Chichi Bridge case on December 14, 2003.[42]

Muhammad Siddiqui was apprehended in South Waziristan on charges of 'committing defiance and for abetting defiance' among the soldiers. He did not disclose the information he had of the Pakistani Air Force personnel plotting to kill General Musharraf. Siddiqui was associated with Shuhada Foundation (established originally by ISI for bereaved soldiers' families' welfare), an organisation of the PAF personnel and other office bearers who wanted to eliminate Musharraf. PAF had no idea that around two dozen personnel at the Chakla air base had been attending meetings with the religious extremists, besides plotting to assassinate General Musharraf. In March 2005, in another trial, death sentence was ruled for Naik Arshad Mehmood and Havaldar Mohammad Younis (Army No. 3060314) of 98 Air Defence Regiment of the army was given a 10 years, rigorous imprisonment. Another accused, Lance Naik Zafar Iqbal Dogar, had earlier abandoned the project and become a state witness.[43]

Besides, on November 19, 2004 an army court sentenced one Mushataq Ahmed to death for inciting six junior officers of the PAF in the above assassination attempt. The officers included chief technician Mehmood, senior technician Karam Din, corporal technician Nawazish Ali, junior technician Niaz Mohammad, Annan Rasheed and Nasrullah. Karam Din and Nasrullah got life imprisonment whereas the rest were given death sentences.[44]

According to *Asia Times,* well placed sources within the Pakistani Army revealed that these officers were arrested after being pinned down by US' FBI for having links with international Islamic militants. Abbasi, a well respected officer, is said to be a very religious person who delivered Quaranic lessons to his junior officers. The report says that the FBI was allowed to establish small cells in the operations offices of the ISI, with ISI officials attached to these cells. Lately, the FBI has been given separate premises all over Pakistan, and its own team of officers, equipped with the best bugging devices in the trade, which allowed it to bust several clandestine activities of Jihadis being undertaken with the connivance of the Pakistan Army.[45]

According to noted journalist Amir Mir, the Pakistan Army is currently divided into two groups—the Islamic fundamentalist Generals and *jawans* and the relatively liberal ones. The speedy trials in army courts and the ruling of severe sentences including death penalty show the seriousness which the army is attaching to the growing influence of the Jihadis among its ranks. It is widely accepted that the assassination attempts on Musharraf could not have been just the handiwork of outsiders and there must have been the involvement of people in General's close circles who are resentful of his U-turn on Afghanistan and Kashmir. There was an intricate web at work encompassing Jihadis groups, the Pakistani Army, the PAF, and the ISI in the Rawalpindi assassination attempt on Musharraf.[46]

Musharraf under Islamists' Influence

In April 2002 General Musharraf held a 'doctored' Referendum to consolidate his position through Jihadis' support since his political base was very slim. Apart from Rawalpindi, maximum turnout was reported from Jhang, where several key militant outfits including Azam Tariq's Sipah-e-Sahba Pakistan (SSP) is based.[47] In the October 2002 elections the army and ISI returned favour to the religious parties enabling the Muttahida Majlis-e-Amal (MMA) to win over 60 seats[48] Prior to elections, the army and ISI have been encouraging the Jihadi groups to join one or the other religious parties, prompting people to join the Jamaat-e-Ulema Islam-Fazl-ur Rehman (JUI-F). Musharraf instructed the provinces to withdraw cases pertaining to violation of electoral code of conduct against ulema and their cadres.[49]

Until the Hisbah Bill was passed, Musharraf largely ignored the MMA's Islamisation drive in the NWFP such as gender segregation in education, introduction of the Sharia laws, banning of music, dance, and NGOs'.[50] Later, he also buckled under pressure on the passport issue. The MMA's protest over the deletion of the religion column in the passports was even supported by the PML-Q Chairman, Chaudhary Shujaat Hussain. The decision to restore the religion column gave the MMA a sense of achievement and proved the level of influence they possessed in the current political dispensation in Pakistan.[51]

Introduced in 1979, during General Zia-ul Haq's tenure the *Hudood* Ordinance prescribed punishment according to Islamic law, such as death penalties, flogging, amputation of limbs, and stoning for theft, adultery and blasphemy.[52] In October 2003, the Pakistan People' Party Parliamentarian (PPPP) moved a bill in the National Assembly calling for the repeal of the *Hudood* Ordinance which was defeated.[53] Prime Minister Jamali assured that no changes would be made in the *Hudood* Ordinance, let alone repealing it.[54] Besides, the government and the MMA had jointly defeated a PML-Q member's bill seeking to put curbs on blasphemy laws and honour killings or *Karo Kari*.[55]

The Necessary Evil?

The shadow of the Jihadis looms large over the present Military regime. Give their key role in Pakistan's jihad based foreign policy in Afghanistan and J&K, the Pakistani establishment has been caught in a dilemma over shutting down their training camps and activities permanently. With the J&K and Afghanistan still far from stable and resolved the Pakistani establishment has a vested interest in keeping them afloat. The roots of the jihadi groups run very deep in the Military establishment and the ISI and the sensitive record of their past collaborative ventures are zealously guarded by the establishment. According to reports, in one incident the army set some records on fire to avoid them from falling into wrong hands or becoming public. The 'fire' was reported to have broken in the army's General Headquarters (GHQ) in Rawalpindi in the section containing secret records of the army and ISI's involvement with the Taliban. Months later, in January 2002, another fire broke out in the 16-storey *Shaheed-e-Millat* secretariat in Islamabad and Indian intelligence sources said that the five hours long fire gutted the administrative and training records pertaining to the Taliban. Indian press reports suggested, "Many of the religious and fundamentalist groups were initially set up by the army to keep the civilian governments of Benazir Bhutto and Nawaz Sharif off balance. In the current context, such records can prove embarrassing. With the two fires, most of the significant records of this dark chapter of Pakistani history may have been eliminated."[56]

The MMA's close link with Jihadis surfaced when Khalid Sheikh Muhammad, the master mind of the September 11 attacks, Omar Saeed Sheikh and Amjad Farooqui were arrested and interrogated. Khalid Sheikh Muhammad was arrested on March 15, 2003, from the house of JI office bearer Ahmed Quddus in Rawalpindi which led to the arrest on the following day of Quddus' uncle Maj. Adil Quddus in NWFP.[57] At the sectarian level, several militants were let off the hook due to MMA's pressure and the crackdowns against sectarian outfits was rendered ineffective due to the MMA's pressure. On some occasions, security agencies' raids on *madaris* were aborted or not undertaken taken at all due to the MMA's pressure on the government. In August 2004, security forces had apprehended two brothers for their terrorist activities who were subsequently released under MMA pressure. The brothers were not only released but charges against them were dropped as well and their government jobs were restored.[58]

The JUI-F, the most influential of the religious parties has been an important component of the federal government's strategy for dealing with the militant in FATA. The government utilised Maulana Fazl-ur Rehman's influence to negotiate with the Mehsud tribe in February 2005.[59] This shows the clout of the leaders like Fazl-ur Rehman and others and the kind of influence they have on these elements.

The fear factor has been a vital part of Jihadis' operations and activities which has to a great extent intimidated the law enforcement officials and even the judges handling their terrorism related cases. Many due to fear for their own lives have preferred to hold trials inside the jails. The fear psychosis surrounding the counter-terrorism efforts has hampered General Musharraf's counter-terrorism strategy. The jihadis have also penetrated among the police ranks which has made General Musharraf's task all the more difficult and complicated.[60] Investigations have revealed the involvement of police personnel in the network of the Jihadis in connection with the assassination attempts on General Musharraf. Hassan Abbas feels that General Musharraf faces an uphill task in his drive against the Jihadis who have developed a massive clout through their links in the political parties, police, intelligence agencies and the Military. He writes:

> "The Pakistan Army dare not confront them, knowing their strength and suspecting that they have many sympathizers, if not supporters, within its own ranks. It was therefore considered more feasible for the army to continue to direct its energies in the battle zone of Kashmir rather than to face the Jihadis. It was for the convenience of its repose that the army, routinely given to having study periods on a myriad of subjects, has apparently not done one on the strength and potential of the Jihadi organizations. No one has clear idea about their exact numbers, but their potential capability resides in the subconciousness of those in authority, and this stays there because the reality of it is too hard to confront."[61]

Chasing Al-Qaida, Ignoring the Taliban

In his book, *In the Line of Fire* General Musharraf claimed that over 689 Al-Qaida operatives have been captured in the global war against terrorism by Pakistan, of which 369 have been handed over to the United States.[62] The prized catch included Abu Zubeida alias Zia-ul Abideen, a Palestinian, Khalid Sheikh Muhammad popularly referred to as KSM, Abu Faraz Al Libbi (regarded as mastermind of attacks on Musharraf), Ammar Al Balochi, Khallad bin Attash and Omar Saeed Sheikh (surrendered). The capture of Al Libbi is considered to be one the greatest feats of the Pakistan Army. The critics of General

Musharraf, however, point out that he has been hunting Al Qaida operatives but going soft on the Taliban fugitives and militia. It has also been alleged that the Pakistan Army has been handing over only the small time Taliban fighters to the United States to keep critics in Washington quiet. The Taliban has become such a formidable foe in the tribal areas that the army is finding it difficult to subdue them completely. The end motive—co-opt them and strike a deal to mutual convenience.

On September 5, 2006 Islamabad struck a deal with the Taliban in the North Waziristan Agency. The text of the deal suggests that the local mujahideen or Taliban were joint signatories along with tribal leaders, elders and Islamabad's political agent. The JUI-F leader Maulana Fazl-ur Rehman, Taliban Commander Mullah Dadullah and Afghan leader Sirajuddin Haqqani are said to have played the key role in working out the deal. Although the deal puts brakes on all Military operations in the area, recommending settlement as per the tribal norms, government sources say that Military action would nonetheless continue to maintain law and order in the area. The killing of Maulana Abdul Kalam and others by the coalition forces in Afghanistan show that the deal had little backing in Afghanistan and that was where it is believed that these kind of contradictions would spell doom for the deal. The Pakistani Army is caught in a dilemma which is getting stronger with unfolding events in not only North Waziristan but South Waziristan as well. Khalid Aziz, former Chief Secretary of the frontier province says that "The agreement is bound to fail as it will add to the Taliban's strength and serve as an opportunity for the coalition forces to launch attacks inside the tribal territories of Pakistan."[63] Since everything has a price, Maulana Fazl-ur-Rehman was rewarded with a deferral of investigations against one of his family members in misappropriation of public funds. Mullah Dadullah and other Taliban leaders have been allowed free movement inside Pakistan to carry on their activities. The government also ignored the activities of the militants led by Haji Mohammad Omar and Baitulla Mehsud in South Waziristan where training and recruiting are in full swing. Also, with the influence of local militant leaders such as Maulana Sadiq Noor, Gul Bahadur and Maulana

Abdul Khaliq being the skeptics and the critics of the deal question the purpose of the deal.[64]

The Jihadi monster which now threatens to unleash its fury on its the masters themselves has come a long way since its creation under General Zia-ul-Haq in the 1970s. Their capacities to inflict considerable damage on the Military and the security apparatus of Pakistan has looked more and more potent in recent years. The have also drawn strengths both the moral and operational support from senior ranking Jihadi-minded Military generals in Muhammad Aziz Khan, Mehmud Ahmed and Hamid Gul, who were once the backbone of the Afghan jihad. Every now and then, they shower praises on Taliban's relentless pursuit of Jihad against the West and pro-West Pakistani government. This may be very upsetting for General Musharraf and his corps commanders. In an interview, General Musharraf himself acknowledged that the influence of the Jihadis in the Army has grown, though in the junior ranks, and there was is a need to check them with an 'iron hand'.[65] The speed of the trials in the army courts and ruling such severe penalties as death show the seriousness that he attaches to this problem. How far would such speedy trials help in containing the growing Jihadi network is yet to be seen.

Conclusion

The main source of the growth of Jihadis has been the politicization of the Military and its nurturing of militant Islam since General Zia's days. General Musharraf had no objection to the Military pursuing such a policy as far as it worked effectively to Pakistan's advantage in Afghanistan and J&K, without any cascading effect on Pakistan. He has definitely gone wrong on this count and failed in his double-edged policy of trying to contain them domestically while giving them freedom to operate in Afghanistan and J&K. The linkage between the Jihadi groups operating in J&K, Afghanistan and at the sectarian level has become the most daunting challenge for General Musharraf. His reliance on the MMA in dealing with the Taliban has not been very successful so far and emboldened the latter on the contrary. The more he undermines democracy, the more difficult it would become for him to contain the Islamist parties and their affiliate

Jihadi groups. He needs the support of the moderate parties and democratic forces if he seeks to reverse the tide of Jihad against Pakistan and his regime. He has to draw support of one of the leading parties, either the PML-N or preferably the PPP to counter the political hold of the Islamist parties and Jihadi groups over Pakistan.

Even though analysts consider the level of influence at the senior level considerably marginal it is still significant enough to create trouble for General Musharraf. Even with 3 per cent senior ranking officers, as per the estimates of Stephen Cohen, heading a corps or undertaking key assignments, can cause enormous damage using the lower ranks which Cohen himself believes is highly infused with fundamentalist ideals. Therefore, the current scale of Jihadi influence on the army, which is minimal for some analysts, must not be dismissed as insignificant. The attacks on General Musharraf and other indicate the magnitude of desperation among the Jihadis to avenge the losses inflicted by General Musharraf's anti-terrorism policies. It would not be totally out of proportion to submit that though General Musharraf can succeed militarily against the Jihadis, it is very unlikely that he would be able to dismantle in a short period, decades-old structures in which the Jihadis have penetrated very deep. He is waging a fight against to alter a system which his own institution has created and in which he was himself was a very active player, not long ago.

NOTES

1. "Sectarianism in Pakistan", *International Crisis Group*, Asia Report No. 95, 18 April 2005, p. 7.
2. Ayesha Jalal, *The State of Martial Rule*. 1990. Cambridge University Press. Cambridge. p. 214.
3. Veena Kukreja, *Contemporary Pakistan. Political Processes, Conflicts and Crises*. 2003. Sage Publications. New Delhi, p. 163.
4. I.A. Rehman, "Generals and the Genie", *Newsline*, April 2005, at http://www.newsline.com.pk/NewsApr2005/cover3apr2005.htm
5. Ibid.
6. A.R. Siddiqi, *The Army In Pakistan: Image and Reality*,

1996.Vanguard, Lahore. pp. 232-233.

7. Brian Cloughley, *A History of the Pakistan Army: Wars and Insurrections*, 1999. Oxford University Press, Oxford. pp. 355-356
8. Stephen P. Cohen, *The Idea of Pakistan*, 2005. Oxford University Press, Oxford, p. 116.
9. Ibid, p. 117.
10. Ibid. 112.
11. Ibid., p. 116
12. "Voices from the Whirlwind: Assessing Musharraf's Predicament", at http://www.pbs.org/frontlineworld/stories/pakistan/a.html
13. Owen Bennett Jones, *Pakistan: Eye of the Storm*. 2002. Yale University Press. New Haven and London. pp. 260-261.
14. Voice from the Whirlwind, No. 12. p. 113.
15. Zahid Hussain, "The Hawk at the Core", *Newsline*, October 2000, p. 21.
16. Ibid.
17. B. Raman, "Why Musharraf Shuffled His Generals", at http://www.rediff.com/news/2004/oct/05raman.htm
18. Ibid.
19. "Gen Mahmud's Exit due to Links with Umar Sheikh" at http://www.dawn.com/2001/10/09/top11.htm. Also see Michael Meacher, *The Guardian*, July 22, 2004.
20. Amir Mateen, "ISI Chief's parleys Continue in Washington", *The News*, September 10, 2001, at http://www.globalreserach.ca/articles/MAT111A.html
21. Jake Tapper, "Spying Eyes and Ears", *Salon*, September 14, 2001, at http://dir.salon.com/politics/feature/2001/09/14/human_spies/index.html.
22. Bob Woodward, *Bush At War*, 2002. Simon & Schuster. New York., p. 47.
23. Tim McGirk, "Rogue No More?", *Time* (Asia), April 29, 2002, at http://www.time.com./time/asia/magazine/article/0,13672,501020506-233999,00.html
24. Interview with Hamid Gul by Arnaud de Borchgrave, United Press International editor at large: Newsweek Web Exclusive, September 14, 2001, at http://globalfire.tv/nj/c2001/politics/wtc.mossad.htm
25. Muhammad Amir Rana, *The Seeds of Terrorism*, New Millennium,

London. 2005, p. 47.

26. There are two factions of JKLF which were born out of the parent organisation called the Jammu Kashmir National Liberation Front (JKNLF) founded in 1977 in the United Kingdom. The faction based in the Pakistan Occupied Kashmir is headed by Amanullah Khan and the one in Indian J&K is headed by Yasin Malik. Through the 1990s, the Malik faction spearheaded Pakistan supported Jihad in J&K until 1996 when he renounced violence to pursue the peaceful route to achieve independence for J&K. At present, the Malik faction is part of the moderates led- All Party Hurriyat Conference in J&K throwing its support behind the India Pakistan peace process.
27. Amir Mir, "Past Imperfect", *Newsline*, July 2005, p. 44.
28. Ibid, p. 46
29. Ibid.
30. See http://timesofindia.indiatimes.com/articlesshow/1702168543.cms
31. "Pakistan Arms Taliban by the Night", *Times of India,* November 1, 2001.
32. "Overt Assistance from Pakistan May Bring Dire Consequences", *Jane's Intelligence Digest*, September 20, 2001, at http:/// www.janes.com/security/international_security/news/jid/jid010920_1_n.shtml.
33. Seymour M. Hersh, "The Gateway", *The New Yorker*, January 21, 2002, at http:www.newyorker.com/fact/content/?020128fa_FACT
34. Tim McGirk, "Rogues No More?", *Time* (Asia), April 2, 2002, at http://www.time.com/time/asia/magazine/article/0,13673,501020506-233999,00.html
35. Ibid.
36. Massoud Ansari, "The Mystery Thickens", *Newsline*, April 2005, p. 36.
37. Syed Shoiab Hasan, "The Whole Truth", *The Herald*, October 2005, p. 34.
38. Rory McCarthy, "Under World where Terror and Security Meet", *The Guardian*, July 16, 2002, at http://www.guardian.co.uk/Archive/Article/0,4273,4462107,00.html
39. Ibid.
40. Zafar Abbas, "What Happened", *The Herald*, June 2005, p. 71.

41. Ibid, p. 75.
42. Amir Mir, "Exit, Extremist Soldier…" *The Herald,* October 2005, p. 64
43. Ibid., p. 65.
44. "Attack on Musharraf: Petition Withdrawn" at http://www.dawn.com./2006/03/16/top17.htm.
45. Syed Saleem Shahzad, "Musharraf's Army Breaking Ranks", *Asia Times,* August 30, 2003, at http://atimes01.atimes.com/atimes/South_Asia/EH30Df01.html
46. Amir Mir, "Musharraf-Jihadi Confrontation Within Army Reaching Boiling Point", at http://www.sattribune.com/archives/200502/p1_mir.htm
47. Strategic Foresight Group. "Window on Pakistan: Rise of Hardliners". *The Times of India,* New Delhi, October 21, 2002.
48. "Case in Point" *The Herald,* December 2002. p. 20.
49. Shamim-ur-Rehman, "Did Govt. Strike Deal with MMA?" at http://www.dawn.com/2002/12/30/top6.htm, accessed January 2, 2003.
50. Ashutosh Misra, "MMA-Democracy Interface in Pakistan: From Natural Confrontation to Forced Co-habitation", *Strategic Analysis,* Vol. 30, No. 2., April-June 2006, p. 390.
51. Amir Siddiqui, "Passport Controversy", *Newsline,* Annual 2005, p. 53.
52. Veena Kukreja, no. 3, p. 172.
53. Shaukat Piracha, "PPPP Moves NA to Repeal Hudood Ord", at http://www.dailytimes.com.pk/default.asp?page=story_16-10-2003_pg1_5.
54. "Qazi Sets Terms for Cooperation: PM Promises No Repeal of Hudood Law", at http://www.dawn.com/2004/03/10/nat3.htm.
55. Raja Asghar, "MMA Joins Govt Against Bill', http://www.dawn.com/2005/03/02/top1.htm.
56. Manoj Joshi, 'Mystery Blaze Erases Pak Army's Jihadi Connection', *The Times of India,* January 17, 2002.
57. Amir Mir, *The True Face of Jehadis: Inside Pakistan Network of Terror,* Roli Books, New Delhi, 2006, p. 26.
58. No. 1, p. 24.
59. Ibid, p. 27.
60. Ibid, pp. 23-24.

61. Hassan Abbas, *Pakistan's Drift into Extremism: Allah, the Army, and America's War on Terror,* 2005, M.E. Sharpe, New York, p. 240.
62. Pervez Musharraf, *In the Line of Fire,* Simon & Schuster, London, 2006, p. 237.
63. Intikhab Amir, "Holes in the Pact", *The Herald*, October 2006, p. 32.
64. Ibid, p. 33.
65. Follow up with Fahad, Geo TV, May 27, 2004, cited in Amir Mir, No. 57, p. 25.

Conclusion

Pakistan's current predicaments can be understood by either studying politicisation of Islam or alternatively Islamization of politics. In both approaches, findings may be fairly similar since the resurgence of Islamists, the dominant theme of this book, was a result of the Military's own attempts at defining Pakistan's identity, political institutions, and foreign policy through the prism of Islam. The interests of Military and the Islamists began to converge due to their common aversion towards democratic principles. The Military was uncomfortable with democracy for it meant a leash on its dominance and decision-making over internal and external affairs. It would make the Military subservient and answerable to people's elected representatives. Similarly, although the Islamists participate in a multiparty democratic set up, they are at odds with democracy when it comes to governance and policy-making. The Islamist parties were vigourously pushing for the implementation of Sharia and adopted a robust Islamisation programme which was seen to be curtailing freedom and rights of people particularly women. Under the Military regimes, the nurturing of militant Islam by the Military for political ends lay the foundation of a working relationship which remains in place till date. Be it the Praetorian regimes or civilian, 'Islam' always remained a principle component of their domestic and foreign policy formulations. General Ayub Khan had to re-declare Pakistan as an Islamic state under pressure form the Ulema and Yahya Khan had to seek their help in countering the Bengali-speaking nationalists in East Pakistan. It emboldened the Islamists and encouraged them to intervene in policy-making from time to time. Similarly, the 1973 Constitution, created under Zulfiqar Ali Bhutto's civilian regime, enshrined extensive Islamic principles to appease the Islamists. Later, under the Military rule of General Zia ul Haq Pakistan's entire socio-political character underwent radical transformation both in policy-making and its implementation. General Zia, a devout Muslim, was eager to carve an Islamic identity for Pakistan and assert its place as the leader in the Islamic world. When Soviet Union invaded Afghanistan in 1979, he got the license to shape Pakistan's political and state institutions in the name of Jihad. *Madaris* mushroomed and militant Islam was exported to Afghanistan and India. So General Zia used Islam for extending Pakistan's area of influence in the region, as much as for legitimising his Praetorian rule. The structures of collaboration between the Military, Jihadis, and the ISI grew stronger under him and as a result saw more and more Islamised officers proliferating in the file and rank of the Military. General Zia not only provided the Islamists with operational and moral power but also legitimized their role in shaping state polices and institution-building.

General Pervez Musharraf, after his coup in October 1999, in spite of being a moderate person, began to incline towards the Islamists because like his predecessors he too was uncomfortable with a strong democratic set-up and political leaders who possessed the potential to push the Military back to the barracks. This brought him closer to the Islamist parties in whom he also saw a willing collaborator for his political machinations. Yet, due to his fundamental character as a moderate person, although he ignored the MMA's agenda for their support in the National Assembly he applied brakes on their Islamisation campaign after a while. The Supreme Court's decision to block the passage of the Hisbah bill and passing amendments in the *Hudood* Ordinance in the National Assembly indicated the limits of his tolerance with Islamization and extremism, yet being able to keep the key MMA constituents in good stead. His cordial relationship with Fazl-ur Rehman had an important role to play the JUI-F's decision to attend the NSC against the wishes of the JI. Likewise, Maulana Fazl-ur Rehman's JUI-F's decision against resigning from the National Assembly in protest against the passing of the *hudood* amendments, despite the pressures from the JI and other MMA constituent parties, reaffirmed General Musharraf's faith in Fazl-ur

Rehman and his party. Over the years the latter has exercised caution while criticizing General Musharraf in the National Assembly and did so only to hoodwink his critics and in cabinet meetings on several occasions he tacitly supported General Musharraf. He played down the tension with the federal government over the FATA operations arguing that it falls under the federal purview.[1] Overall, as a strong Deobandi figure Fazl-ur-Rehman's standing remains undisputed and he remains the central figure for the Centre in tackling not only the Shia factor at the sectarian level but also the Taliban in the FATA region and the drive for regulating madaris in the NWFP. He was the federal government's key interlocutor in facilitating the September 2006 deal with the Taliban in North Waziristan.

The main worry for the MMA in the next elections remains to be its unity which was a critical component of its unprecedented victory in 2002 elections. A fractured MMA in practical terms may not impact much on its prospects with JUI-F and JI being the key parties which are still running the show but the detachment of other constituents like the JUP, JUI-S, JAH and PIT from the MMA may have a demoralising affect on the MMA supporters and help the mainstream parties make in-roads into their political domain. What the MMA requires is at least harmonisation of relations and interest between the JUI-F and JI. Belonging to the most influential Sunni sect (Deobandi) in Pakistan and having the largest number of *Madaris*, the JUI-F is a powerful socio-politico-religious force to reckon with in the NWFP and Balochistan and gaining in strengths in other provinces as well. Whereas the JI possesses a larger cadre base in Pakistan, controls local government in Sindh and is politically active in Punjab and NWFP. Such strong bases having combined in the next elections may brighten the party's chances considerably.

The other concern for the MMA is to undo its past mistakes and retain some of its lost credibility caused by the 'deal' with General Musharraf over the LFO. The deal struck twin blows on the MMA. It subjected it to public criticism on the one hand and alienated the ARD parties on the other. The MMA has also been accused of adopting double standards by remaining in the coalition in Balochistan, even while criticising the Military operations in the FATA and Balochistan. The ARD categorically conveyed it to the MMA that it should resign from the government in Balochistan and objected to the MMA raising Islamic slogans and personal issues during joint protests against the government. The PPPP demanded the MMA to support the ARD over the scraping of the 17th Amendment, restoration of democracy and parliamentary supremacy and holding early free and fair elections in 2005.[2] The MMA's parliamentary leader, Qazi Hussein Ahmed's articulated the party's response saying that its struggle would go with or without the ARD and reiterated that the MMA did demand the resignation of General Musharraf, restoration of the Constitution and the supremacy of the Parliament.[3] On the question of fresh elections he said that it can only be considered provided the PPPP promised to support the MMA candidates in the next elections.[4] The response indicated the MMA's bid to carve an identity for itself and not get dictated by the ARD-constituent parties and their political agenda. A worried MMA keen to resurrect its image has been taking steps towards that end. It sensibly entered into a four-point agreement with the federal government over the registration of foreigners in FATA which showed a more moderate character of the party. Also, the NWFP government's decision to start registering the *madaris* in the province improved the parties public image outside the NWFP.

The MMA has also been engaged in hectic parleys with the ARD hoping that it may also help improve its democratic bonafide. In 2004-05 unsuccessful parleys between the MMA and ARD showed the former's desperation to burry the hatchet with the latter for political gains. In October 2004 Maulana Fazl-ur-Rehman visited Nawaz Sharif in Jeddah in Saudi Arabia to express his condolences over the demise of the latter's father. During the meeting the two leaders had touched upon domestic issues also. Later, on February 10, 2005, Sajid Mir, leader of *Jamiat Ahle Hadith* also visited Jeddah to talk about an MMA-PML-N joint protest from April 2005. During the meeting, Nawaz Sharif is reported to have conveyed his willingness to meet Qazi Hussain Ahmed and Fazl-ur Rehman to discuss the prospects of such a front.[5] Eventually the meeting materialized when Qazi Hussain Ahmed met Nawaz Sharif on February 25, 2005. In the meeting the two leaders agreed over launching a joint struggle against the government, but Nawaz Sharif also expressed his disappointment over MMA's support to the 17th Amendment.[6] Fazl-ur Rehman met Nawaz Sharif, on February 26 and discussed the possibility of a joint front against the government.[7] In a significant development on February 10, 2005 Nawaz Sharif and Benazir Bhutto also held talks in Jeddah. The last time they met was in 1988 in Pakistan.[8] In the Jeddah meeting the PPPP leader refrained from discussing any kind of alliance prospects with the MMA and confined its discussions to the need to restore the 1973 Constitution which showed PPPP's apprehension toward PML-N's historic relationship with the *ulema*.[9] Nonetheless, should the MMA come under the wings of the ARD before the next elections it can seriously upset PML-Q election prospects.

The biggest challenge however, to the ruling PML-Q and the military controlled political system comes from the moderate parties and they have shown signs of a combined opposition. In June 2006, in a landmark progress towards forming a common front against the Military regime, the PPPP and PML-N agreed to a 36-point Charter of Democracy, the so called Magna Carta of Pakistan. The document addresses pressing problems confronting the Pakistani politics since several decades, some of which ironically had been created by the leading architects of the Charter themselves. The Charter declares: "The Military dictatorship and the nation cannot co-exist as Military involvement adversely affects the economy and the democratic institutions as well as the defence capabilities and integrity of the country...the nation needs new direction, different from militaristic and regimental approach of the Bonapartist regimes, as the current one".[10] The Charter consists of four parts namely, constitutional amendments, code of conduct, free and fair elections and civil-Military relations, with an emphasis on making Prime Minister the real chief executive with full powers and authority; clear rules and guidelines for the selection of Chief Election Commissioner and Chief Justice and judges of the superior courts. The Charter calls for restoring the 1973 Constitution and the repeal of the LFO and the 17th Amendment baring the provisions related to the creation of a joint electorate, reserved seats from women and minorities and lowering of the voting age. The Charter wants the powers to appoint the Governor, three Service chiefs (one of the factors in the overthrow of civilian governments) and the Chairman Joint Chiefs of Staff Committee to rest in the Prime Minister. For the selection of the Election Commissioner and the Commission's other members, the Charter recommends a decision-making mechanism consisting of leaders of the opposition, representatives from the legal field and parliamentary committee with equal representation of opposition and treasury benches.[11]

As far as code of conduct is concerned the Charter firmly supports the Abolishing of the National Security Council and revival of Defence Committee of the Cabinet having representatives from the three services, under the Prime Minister. It also seeks to abolish the National Accountability Bureau and instead creation of "an independent commission whose chairman would be nominated by the Prime Minister and in Consultation with the leader of the opposition and confirmation from a joint parliamentary committee.[12] Significantly, wary of political leaders approving of Military takeovers in the past, to get even with political adversaries, the Charter debars the signatories of the charter from joining a Military regime or any Military-sponsored government. It can only be regarded as wishful thinking and difficult to practice in politics wherein craving for power, prestige and money defies all norms and principles of human behaviour. Would the PPPP supreme Benazir Bhutto be able to resist a deal with General Musharraf which enables here return and ascent to power? Then would only this Charter be put for its litmus test. Quite rightly, sceptics questions about the code of ethics for the politicians themselves who in the past have run to align and conspire with the Military to oust their political opponents at the slightest opportunity. Plus, how glorious has been the 'democratic past' of the country that the people should feel encouraged by the Charter's promise?[13] Are the moderate parties ready to follow the norms in letter and spirit themselves which they look for others to follow? Although the Charter on this count does hold the political parties responsible for the mess that democracy in Pakistan finds in today, yet it remains vulnerable to the likelihood of the code of conduct being dumped at the slightest possibility of a political deal with the Military.

Another major area of concern addressed in the Charter is the domineering role of the ISI in politics and governance which significantly narrows down their domestic political space and autonomy. The Charter recommends need for making the intelligence agencies accountable to strengthen and stabilise democratic regimes and governance in the long run. The Charter says: "The ISI, the MI (Military Intelligence) and other security agencies shall be accountable to the elected government through the Prime Minister's secretariat, the Ministry of Defence and the cabinet division." It also calls for disbanding the political wings of the intelligence agencies and putting their budget under the control of the Defence Committee of the Cabinet. Also mentioned is the reforming of the armed forces and investigating its vast corporate network and investments in Pakistan for alleged corruption and malpractices.[14]

In the run-up to the next elections General Musharraf put the brakes on the Islamisation drive of the MMA to come clear of his past dealing with them. He has consciously started to pursue his policy of enlightened moderation to project his regime as progressive and moderate. He has made sure that the local governments are under his control and play their due role in the next elections. But before the next general elections he will have to get himself re-elected, since his tenure expires in December 2007. For this he will have to seek re-election by the current assemblies by October or November and then hold the general elections. The biggest problem though which General Musharraf faces is that his former political allies, the MMA is plotting his ouster, and the ARD parties' led opposition gathering more steam. He would need support from the moderate parties and for this a pre-election understanding or 'deal' becomes necessary. There is a possibility to enter into a political understanding with the PPPP, by assuring Benazir Bhutto that she and her husband would be freed of all their charges and allowed to contest provided they supported his re-election in the current assemblies. Should the PPPP come to power it would be obliged to endorse his re-election, just as the MMA had done in 2004. Such a deal is possible more with the PPPP than with the PML-N, for the reasons discussed in the previous chapters. The only possible hindrance to any deal would be his uniform and it seems that the PPPP would certainly not enter into any understanding without any promise from him to relinquish his uniform. While the chances of Benazir Bhutto to return to Pakistan are getting stronger, the question to be asked is what would it mean for the ruling PML-Q and PML-N? The hardest hit would be the PML-Q who since 2002 has been Pervez Musharraf's own bet. They would be asked to prepare for their exit from the corridors of power. Would they or would they resent? How would they react to Benazir Bhutto being given power on a platter? Certainly, the PML-Q leadership led by Chaudhary Shujaat Hussein would be looking for ways to tackle the Benazir factor. Would Benazir Bhutto's return prompt Nawaz Sharif to return and take on General Musharraf and his PML-Q regime? Chances are that he would try all means available to re-enter politics. This would be a welcome development for democracy though unpleasant for the PML-Q which may witness a reverse exodus of its members of their parent party, under Nawaz Sharif. Equally important is the question of how the Jihadis would take Benazir Bhutto's return to Pakistan and help strengthen democracy? How would the Islamised segments in the ISI and the Military react to her comeback? She certainly is not good news for them if she offers the promise of a strong democracy, checks on the workings of the ISI as per the Charter and curbs on sectarianism and extremism. At present both General Musharraf and the PPPP seem inclined to get into a partnership to help stabilize Pakistan and curtail extremist tendencies and threats to the country. General Musharraf in his book *In the Line of Fire* has called the next elections as the 'mother of all elections' and expressed his resolve to defeat the MMA at all costs. The prospective partnership with the PPPP puts the Military-Islamist engagement under severe stress. Pervez Musharraf for himself being target of the Jihadi attacks in the past has shown resolve in checking their growth but without much success. The influence and linkages of the Jihadis in the ISI and the Military still continues to challenge his writ and policy of enlightened moderation. Many retired and serving Generals are believed to be highly Islamised in thinking and maintain their links with the Jihadi groups. If the Military leaves the political centrestage, without having established a credible counter-balancing democratic dispensation, it may spell chaos for Pakistan. Therefore, for Pakistan it is absolutely essential that next elections are free and fair and the government which comes to power, whether under Benazir Bhutto or someone else, is seen people's genuine representative rather than the Military's representative.

NOTES

1. Ejaz Haider, "The Political Chessboard", *The Friday Times*, February 18-24, 2005.
2. Asim Yasin, "PPP has Reservations About ARD-MMA Alliance" at http://www.jang.com.pk/thenews/feb2005-daily/18-02-2005/metro/i2.htm
3. 'MMA Struggle to Continue With or Without ARD Cooperation: Qazi', at http://www.jang.com.pk/thenews/mar2005-daily/07-03-2005/metro/l2.htm
4. Mohammad Imran, "MMA Sets Conditions for Support to ARD" at http://www.dailytimes.com.pk/default.asp?page=story_23-2-2005_pg7_13
5. Muhammand Faisal Ali, "Mir, Nawaz Discuss 17th Amend" at http://pakobserver.net/200502/01/news/topstories05.asp
6. Amir Wasim, "Nawaz, Qazi Agree to Launch Joint Anti-Govt. Drive" at http://dawn.com/2005/01/26/top3.htm
7. "Fazl, Nawaz Discuss Cooperation" at http://www.dawn.com/2005/01/27/top1.htm
8. "Benazir Meets Nawaz" at http://nation.com.pk/daily/feb-2005/11/index1.php
9. See no. 77.
10. Zaffar Abbas, "Great Expectations", *The Herald*, June 2006, p. 36.
11. Ibid, p. 37.
12. Ibid.
13. Amir Zia, "Charter of Hope?", *Newsline*, June 2006, p. 42.

Appendices

Appendix I

Party Positions in National Assembly (As of June 2004)

Pakistan Muslim League (PML)	
Pakistan Muslim League-Quaid-e-Azam (PML-Q)	128
National Alliance (NA)	015
Pakistan Muslim League-Functional (PML-F)	005
Pakistan Muslim League-Jinnah (PML-J)	003
Pakistan Muslim League-Zia (PML-Z)	001
Total	**152**
PML Allies	
Muttahida Qaumi Movement (MQM)	016
Pakistan People's Party-Patriot (PPP-P)	017
Pakistan Awami Tehrik (PAT)	001
Pakistan People's Party-Sherpao (PPP-S)	002
Federally Administered Tribal Areas (FATA)	007
Total	**043**
Alliance for Restoration for Democracy (ARD) and Allies	
Pakistan People's Party Parliamentarian (PPPP)	058
Pakistan Muslim League-Nawaz (PML-N)	018
Balochistan National Party (BNP)	001
Jamhoori Watan Party (JWP)	001
Pakistan Tehrik-e-Insaaf (PTI)	001
Pakhtoonkhwa Milli Awami Party (PkMAP)	001
Total	**080**
Muttahida Majlis-e-Amal (MMA) and FATA Allies	
MMA	060
FATA	005
Total	**065**

Source: *Daily Times*, June 29, 2004 at http://www.dailytimes.com.pk/default.asp?page=story_29-6-2004_pg7_46

Appendix II

Party Positions in the Senate (As of February 2003)

PML-Q	035
MMA	018
PPPP	011
MQM	006
PML-N	004
NA	003
PPP-Sherpao	002
PkMAP	002
ANP	002
PML-F	001
BNP-Awami	001
BNP-Mengal	001
Balochistan National Movement (BNM)	001
JWP	001
Independent	004
Independent (FATA)	008
Total	**100**

Source: *State of Democracy Report, Revival of Democracy-1st year of Democracy*, November 16, 2002-November 15, 2003, Pakistan Institute for Legislative Development and Transparency (PILDAT).

Appendix III

Major Party Positions in the Provincial Assemblies (As of January 2003)

Punjab Provincial Assembly	
PML-Q	216
PPPP	065
PML-N	043
NA	016
MMA	011
PPP-Patriots	008
PML-J	005
Sindh Provincial Assembly	
PPPP	062
MQM	041
PML-Q	018
NA	016
PML-F	013
MMA	008
NWFP Provincial Assembly	
MMA	066
PML-Q	010
PPP-Sherpao	013
PPPP	010
ANP	010
PML-N	005
Independent	007
Balochistan Provincial Assembly	
PML-Q	021
MMA	018

Source: *State of Democracy Report, Revival of Democracy-1st year of Democracy*, November 16, 2002-November 15, 2003, Pakistan Institute for Legislative Development and Transparency (PILDAT).

Appendix IV
The MMA Manifesto

Muttahida Majlis-e-Amal has released its 15-point manifesto. The detailed party programme would be made public later.

The main points of the manifesto are as under:

> *To revive fear of God, affection to the Prophet (PBUH) and service to people with particular emphasis on government officials and cabinet members.*

- To make Pakistan a true Islamic welfare state to ensure justice to people and eradicate corruption whatsoever.
- To ensure provision of bread, clothes, shelter, education, jobs and marriage expenses to all citizens.
- To protect basic human rights (life, property and honour) of citizens.
- To create an independent, just and humane economic system where citizens will be provided opportunities for halal jobs, business and investments.
- To ensure uniform and quick justice to every citizen, from the president to a layman.
- To develop a God fearing, helping, brave and protecting police system.
- To get the entire society literate within ten years to enable everyone to know one's rights and responsibilities.
- To ensure compulsory and free of charge education till matriculation and provide opportunities to meritorious students and scholars for advanced research.
- To protect rights of women guaranteed by Islam and restoration of their honour and prestige.
- To abolish all chronic and new feudal system with forfeiture of illegal wealth and its distribution among poor.

- To provide lands to peasants and formers for their livelihood and guarantee reasonable prices to their produce.
- To protect provincial autonomy and district governments, taking care of backward areas and classes and taking special steps to get them at par with developed areas.
- To get the country and people rid of influence of imperialistic forces and their local agents.
- To extend moral, political and diplomatic help and support to all suppressed with particular emphasis on Kashmiris, Palestinians, [1] Afghans and Chechnyans.

Source: http://mma.org.pk/the.party/manifesto/

References

Books

Abbas, Hassan, *Pakistan's Drift into Extremism: Allah, the Army, and America's War on Terror*, M.E. Sharpe. New York. 2005.

——, *Poleaxe of Politics of the Eighth Amendment 1985-1997*, Watandost, Lahore, 1997.

Ahmed, Talmiz, *Islamic Groups and Movements in India*. Author's Publications. 2001.

Jalal, Ayesha, *Democracy and Authoritarianism in South Asia: A Comparative and Historical Perspective*. Cambridge University Press; Cambridge. 1995.

——, *The State of Martial Rule: The Origins of Pakistan's Political Economy of Defence*, Cambridge University Press. Cambridge. 1990.

Cloughley, Brian, *A History of the Pakistan Army: Wars and Insurrections*, Oxford University Press, Oxford. 1999.

Cohen, Stephen P., *The Idea of Pakistan*, Oxford University Press, Oxford, 2005.

Dixit, J.N. Dixit, *India-Pakistan in War and Peace*. 2002. Books Today; New Delhi, 2002.

Esposito, John L. and John O. Voll, *Islam and Democracy*, Oxford University Press, Oxford, 1996.

Grover, Verinder and Ranjana Arora (ed.), *Political System in Pakistan*, Deep and Deep Publications, New Delhi, 1995.

Haqqani, Husain, *Pakistan: Between Mosque and Military*, Vanguard Books, Lahore, 2005.

Hussain, Mushahid and Akmal Hussain, *Pakistan, Problem of Governance*. Konark Publishers, New Delhi. 1993.

Jones, Owen Bennett, *Pakistan: Eye of the Storm*, Yale University Press. New Haven and London, 2002.

Kukreja, Veena, *Contemporary Pakistan: Political Processes, Conflicts and Crises*, Sage Publications, New Delhi, 2003.

Mai, Mukhtar, *In the Name of Honour: A Memoir* (translated in English by Marie Therese Cuny), Atria Books, New York, 2006.

Mir, Amir, *The True Face of Jehadis: Inside Pakistan Network of Terror*, Roli Books, New Delhi, 2006.

Musharraf, Pervez, *In the Line of Fire: A Memoir*, Simon & Schuster, London, 2006.

Nordlinger, Eric A., *Soldiers in Politics Military Coups and Governments*, Prentice-Hall, New Jersey, 1977.

Rana, Muhammad Amir, *The Seeds of Terrorism*, New Millennium, London. 2005.

Rizvi, Hasan Askari, *The Military and Politics in Pakistan 1947-86*, Konark Publisher, New Delhi, 1988.

Siddiqa, Ayesha, Military Inc, *Inside Pakistan's Military Economy*, Pluto Press. London. 2007.

Siddiqi, A.R., *The Army in Pakistan: Image and Reality*, 1996. Vanguard, Lahore

Talbot, Ian, *Pakistan: A Modern History*, Oxford University Press, New Delhi, 1998.

Woodward, Bob, *Bush at War*, 2002. Simon & Schuster. New York.

Journal Articles

Abbas, Zafar, "What Happened", *Herald*, June 2005.

——, "Full Circle", *Herald*, November 1999

——, "Great Expectations", *Herald*, June 2006.

Akhtar, Aasim Sajjad, "Fauji's Foundation", *Himal*, 16/11, November 2003.

Alvi, Hamza, "Ethnicity, Muslim Society, and the Pakistan Ideology", in Anita M. Weiss, ed., *Islamic Reassertion in Pakistan*, Syracuse University Press, Syracuse, 1986.

Amir, Intikhab, "Holes in the Pact", *Herald*, October 2006.

Ansari, Massoud, "The Battle for Balochistan", *Newsline*, September 2006.

——, "The Militarization of Pakistan", *Newsline*, October 2004.

——, "The Mystery Thickens", *Newsline*, April 2005.

——, "The Numbers Game", *Newsline*, October 2004.

Askari, Hussain, "Another Muttahida". *Herald.* November 2002.

Hasan, Syed Shoiab, "Battle Front Sui", *Herald*, February 2005.

——, "The Whole Truth", *Herald*, October 2005.

Hussain, Zahid, "A Military State", *Newsline*, October 2004.

——, "The Hawk at the Core", *Newsline*, October 2000.

Khan, Azizullah, "Wining to Lose," *Herald*, February 2005.

Khan, M. Ilyas, "Inside the MMA," *Herald.* November 2002.

——, "Interview with Qazi Hussain Ahmed", *Herald.* November 2002.

Mir, Amir, "Exit, Extremist Soldier...", *Herald*, October 2005.

——, "Past Imperfect", *Newsline*, July 2005.

Misra, Ashutosh, "MMA-Democracy Interface in Pakistan: From Natural Confrontation to Forced Co-habitation", *Strategic Analysis*, Vol. 30, No. 2, April-June 2006.

——, "Rise of Islamist parties in Pakistan: Causes and Prospects", *Strategic Analysis*, Vol. 27, No. 2, April-June 2003.

Rizvi, Hasan Askari, "Civil Military Relations in Contemporary Pakistan", *Survival*, Vol. 40, No. 2, Summer 1998.

Siddiqa, Ayesha, "Soldiers of Fortune", *Newsline*, December 2006.

Siddiqui, Amir, "Passport Controversy", *Newsline*, Annual 2005.

Tohid, Owais, "Backward March", *Newsline*, July 2003.

——, "The Sound of Silence", *Newsline*, July 2003.

Zaidi, Mubashir, "State of Confusion", *Herald*, February 2005.

Zia, Amir, "Charter of Hope?", *Newsline*, June 2006.

Zia, Shiraz. "Media", *Herald.* November 2002.

"Case in Point", *Herald.* December 2002.

Website References

Ahmed, Khaled, "Will Qazi Hussain Ahmed Stop Basant Next Year?" at www.thefridaytimes.com/main31.htm.

Ahmed, Mutahir, "MMA's victory: Implications for Pakistan", at http://www.jang.com.pk/thenews/oct2002-weekly/nos-20-10-2002/pol1.htm.

Ahmed, Waseem, "MMA MPA Seeks Law Against Music, Women's Photos in Ads.", at http://www.dawn.com/2005/02/04/top7.htm.

Ali, Ghafar, "Centre has Lifted Ban on Madrassa Registration" at http:/

/www.dailytimes.com.pk/default.asp?page=story_25-7-2004_pg7_36.

Ali, Muhammand Faisal, "Mir, Nawaz Discuss 17th Amend" at http://pakobserver.net/200502/01/news/topstories05.asp.

Ali, Zulfiqar, "Fazl Accuses General Musharraf of Supporting PPP" at http://www.dawn.com/2005/03/29/top2.htm.

Amin, Akhtar, "14 Peshawar UC Nazims Resign in Protest" at http://www.jang-group.com/thenews/may2004-daily/05-05-2004/national/n4.htm.

Asghar, Raja and Ahmed Hassan, "Dual Office Bill Passed Amid Protests" at http://www.dawn.com/2004/10/15/top4.htm.

Ashgar, Raja, "Senate Passes Women's Bill; MMA Amendments Rejected", at http://www.dawn.com/2006/11/24/top1.htm.

——, "Some Respite for Women, at Last: Protection of Rights Bill Gets through NA", at http://www.dawn.com/2006/11/16/top1.htm.

——, "General Musharraf Wins Vote of Confidence" at http://www.dawn.com/2004/01/02/top1.htm.

——, "MMA joins Govt Against Bill" at http://www.dawn.com/2005/03/02/top1.htm.

——, "NA Adopts NSC Bill Amid Uproar: MQM Amendments Incorporated" at http://www.dawn.com/2004/04/08/top1.htm.

——, "NA Prorogued Amid Protests: No Business on Third Day" at http://www.dawn.com/2002/03/11/nat.htmMarch 11, 2003.

——, "Opposition Cries Foul As NSC Bill is Passed" at http://www.dawn.com/2004/04/15/top1.htm.

——, "Opposition's NA Session on Bugti", at http://www.dawn.com/2006/08/29/top5.htm.

——, "PML-Q, MMA Win Majority Seats" at http://www.dawn.com/2003/01/17/top1.htm.

——, "Senate Passes Twin-Office Bill Amid Protests" at http://www.dawn.com/2004/11/02/top1.htm.

Bokhari, Jawaid, "World Bank for Land Reforms", on http://www.dawn.com/2002/11/13/ebr4.htm.

Bukhari, Mubasher, "PA Resolution demands Musharraf keep Uniform", at http://www.dailytimes.com.pk/print.asp?page=story_14-9-2004_pg1_3&ndate=09/16/2004%201:16:48%20PM.

Chaudhary, Ghani, "Women in Pak Elections", on http://www.dailymirror.lk/2002/10/16/opinion/3.html.

Hasan, Ahmed and Amir Wasim, "Cabinet Wants Musharraf to Keep Both Posts; President will Agree, Hopes Rashid", at http://www.dawn.com/2004/09/16/top1.htm.

Hasan, Ahmed, "MMA to 'Resign' in December", at http://www.dawn.com/2006/11/17/top3.htm.

——, "MMA, Govt. Sign Deal: Govt. Sacking to be Referred to SC, NSC Formation Through Parliament, No Extension in Superior Court Judges" Retirement Age' at http://www.dawn.com/2003/12/25/top2.htm.

Hassnain, Zakir, "NWFP PA Rejects Amendments to Hudood Ord" at http://www.dailytimes.com.pk/default.asp?page=story_10-9-2003_pg7_8.

——, "Opposition Calls *Hisbah* Martial Law of Mullas" at http://www.dailytimes.com.pk/default.asp?page=story_27-8-2003_pg7_27.

——, "PM to Open BoK Islamic Banking Branch Tomorrow" at http://www.dailytimes.com.pk/default.asp?page=story_21-11-2003_pg7_38.

Hersh, Seymour M., "The Gateway", *The New Yorker*, January 21, 2002, at http:www.newyorker.com/fact/content/?020128fa_FACT.

Imran, Mohammad, "Centre Planning Law to Register Seminaries" at www.dailytimes.com.pk/default. asp?page=story_28-2-2005_pg1_3.

——, "MMA Sets Conditions for Support to ARD" at http://www.dailytimes.com.pk/default.asp?page=story_23-2-2005_pg7_13.

"Interview with Hamid Gul" by Arnaud de Borchgrave, United Press International editor at large: Newsweek Web Exclusive, September 14, 2001, at http://globalfire.tv/nj/c2001/politics/wtc.mossad.htm.

Iqbal, Nasir, "Hasba Clauses Ruled Contrary to Constitution: NWFP Governor may not Assent to Law: SC" at http://www.dawn.com/2005/08/05/top1.htm.

——, "SC Moved Against Hasba Bill", at http://www.dawn.com/2006/11/16/top9.htm.

Jabbar, Qamar, "MMA Divided Over Attending NSC Meeting" at http://www.dailytimes.com.pk/default.asp?page=story_16-2-2005_pg7_14.

Kaiser Bengali, "Perils of Militarised Politics", at Pakistan People's Party website at http://www.ppp.org.pk/dfc/kaiserbengali.html. Originally published at http://www.dawn.com/2006/08/03/op.htm#1.

Khan, Bahzad Alam, "MMA in Do-or-die Talks", at http:www.dawn.com/2006/12/07/top2.htm.

Khan, Ismail Khan, "JUI-F Approach to the NSC" at http://www.http://www.dawn.com/2005/03/09/top4.htm.

Khan, Khurram Dastgir, "The Coming Theocracy" at http://www.jang.com.pk/thenews/nov2002-daily/02-11-2002/oped/o2.htm.

Khattak, Iqbal, "MMA Impending District Governments in NWFP" at http://www.dailytimes.com.pk/default.asp?page=story_9-1-2003_pg7_26.

——, "MMA Takes Unconstitutional Step with Sharia, *Hisbah* Bills" at http://www.thefridaytimes.com/inews6a.htm.

Mateen, Amir, "ISI Chief's parleys Continue in Washington", *The News*, September 10, 2001, at http://www.globalreserach.ca/articles/MAT111A.html.

McCarthy, Rory, "Under World where Terror and Security Meet", *The Guardian*, July 16, 2002, at http://www.guardian.co.uk/Archive/Article/0,4273,4462107,00.html.

McGirk, Tim, "Rogue No More?", *Time* (Asia), April 29, 2002, at http://www.time.com./time/asia/magazine/article/0,13672,501020506-233999,00.html.

Mehmood, Amjad, "MMA Marchers Condemn Attack", on http://www.dawn.com/2003.03/24/top3.htm.

Mir, Amir, "Musharraf-Jihadi Confrontation Within Army Reaching Boiling Point", at http://www.sattribune.com/archives/200502/p1_mir.htm.

Mughal, Muhammad Aamir, "Unemployment in Pakistan & Army-2", at http://www.forum.atimes.com/topic.asp? Topic_ID=982, posted on 03'29/2005.

Najeeb, Muhammad, "Pakistan Opposition Questions Anti-terror Raid" at http://www.southasiamonotor.org/pak/2004/sept/10pak2.html.

Piracha, Shaukat, "PPPP Moves NA to Repeal *Hudood* Ord", at http://www.dailytimes.com.pk/default.asp?page=story_16-10-2003_pg1_5.

Qadir, Shaukat, "Pakistani Islamists Stage Anti-US Demonstration", at http://www.naviquest.com/812313459.htm.

Qazi, Reza Rehman Khan, "The Political Economy of MMA's Victory", at http://www.jang.com.pk/thenews/oct2002-weekly/nos-20-10-2002/pol1.htm#6.

Rais, Rasul Baksh, "Rise of Islamist Parties", *The News.* October 19, 2002 at www.jang.com.pk/thenews/oct2002-daily/ 19-10-2002/oped/opinion.htm.

Raman, B., "Why Musharraf Shuffled His Generals", at http://www.rediff.com/news/2004/oct/05raman.htm.

——, "Islamisation of Pakistan's Economy". September 30, 2000, on http://www.asiafeatures.com/business/0010,1505,03.html.

Raza, Shehzada, "No Let-up in Tribal Offensive, Says Faisal" at http://www.dailytimes.com.pk/default.asp?page=story_19-3-2004_pg7_26.

Raza, Syed Irfan, "Nadra to Issue Passports with Religion from Today", at http://www.dawn.com/2005/03/28/top3.htm.

Rehman, I.A., "Generals and the Genie", *Newsline*, April 2005, at http://www.*Newsline*.com.pk/NewsApr2005/cover3apr2005.htm.

Rehman, Shamim-ur, "Did Govt. Strike Deal with MMA?" at http://www.dawn.com/2002/12/30/top6.htm.

——, "Sindh PA Supports President in Uniform", at http://www.dawn.com/2004/09/03/top3.htm.

Riaz, Mohammed, "NWFP Adopts Islamic Morality Bill: Opposition Calls it 'Maulvi's Martial Law", at http://www.dawn.com/2006/11/14/top1.htm.

——, "NWFP PA Passes the Hasbah Bill", at http://www.dawn.com/2005/07/15/top1.htm.

——, "Musharraf Should Quit One Office: Frontier PA", at http://www.dawn.com/2004/09/16/top3.htm.

Rizvi, Hasan Askari, "Musharraf's Army Uniform", at http://www.dailytimes.com.pk/default.asp?page=story_13-9-2004_pg3_2.

Shahid, Saleem, "Bugti Killed in Operation: Six Officers among 21 Security Personnel Dead", at http://www.dawn.com/2006/08/27/top1.htm.

Shahzad, Syed Saleem, "Musharraf's Army Breaking Ranks", *Asia Times*, August 30, 2003, at http://atimes01.atimes.com/atimes/South_Asia/EH30Df01.html.

Shakeer, Naeem, "The Blasphemy Law in Pakistan and its Impact", on http://www.ahrchk.net/hrsolid/mainfile.php/1999vol09no07/1143/.

Shehzad, Muhhammad, "General Musharraf's Biggest Quandry: The On-going Waziristan Resistance" at http://www.satribune.com/archives/nov04/P1_msh.htm.

Siddiqi, Safdar Hasan, "Building Quaid-e-Azam's Pakistan", on http://www.insaf.org.pk/articles/articles_building_Quaid-e-Azams_Pakistan.htm.

Sreedhar, T. "Pakistan's Economic Dilemma". at http://www.nyu.edu/globalbeat/southasia/06181998sreedhar1.html

Staff Correspondent, "Benazir Meets Nawaz" at http://nation.com.pk/daily/feb-2005/11/index1.php

——, "Foreigners Registration", *The News*, July 8, 2004 at http://www.infopak.gov.pk/writeups/foreigner's_reg.htm

——, "MMA Legislators Infuriated Over Wana Operations" at http://www.jang.com.pk/the news/mar2004-daily/18-03-2004/metro/k4.htm

——, "MMA Struggle to Continue With or Without ARD Cooperation: Qazi", at http://www.jang.com.pk/thenews/mar2005-daily/07-03-2005/metro/l2.htm

Staff Reporter, "Attack on Musharraf: Petition Withdrawn" at http://www.dawn.com./2006/03/16/top17.htm.

——, "Aziz Wins Both Seats by Huge Margins", at http://www.dawn.com/2004/08/19/top1.htm.

——, "Fazl, Nawaz Discuss Cooperation" at http://www.dawn.com/2005/01/27/top1.htm

——, "Freedom of Voice" on http://www.dawn.com/2002/10/22ed.htm.

——, "Gen Mahmud's Exit due to Links with Umar Sheikh" at http://www.dawn.com/2001/10/09/top11.htm.

——, "General Musharraf Appoints Khalilur Rehman as New Governor NWFP" at http://pakistantimes.net/2005/03/13/top3.htm

——, "Govt. Submits Reply in Pleas Against 17th Amendment" at http://www.dawn.com/2005/03/28/nat1.htm.

——, "Hudood Laws will be Amended, and not Repealed" at http://www.dawn.com/2006/07/18/top7.htm

——, "JUI-F Calls for End to NSC Boycott" at http://www.dawn.com/2005/03/07/top4.htm

——, "MMA Criticizes Plan for New Cantonments", at http://www.dawn.com/2005/02/23/nat9.htm.

——, "MMA March: Durrani Vetoes Nazim's Order" at http://www.dawn.com/2005/03/28/nat7.htm.

——, "MMA to Enforce Shariat Laws" at www.dawn.com/2002/10/17/nat8.htm.

——, "MMA to Fulfill Pledges Made to World: Leaders Assure Diplomats" at http://www.dawn.com/2002/10/24/top2.htm.

——, "MPA for Ban on Basant" at http://www.dawn.com/2003/02/04/nat14.htm.

——, "Opposition Cries Foul on Rashid's Remarks: Musharraf's Army's Post", at http://www.dawn.com/2004/09/16/top2.htm.

——, "PML Launches Drive Against Referendum" at http://www.dawn.com/2002/04/13/nat3.htm.

——, "PML Launches Drive Against Referendum" at http://www.dawn.com/2002/04/13/nat3.htm.

——, "Qazi Sets Terms for Cooperation: PM Promises No Repeal of *Hudood* Law" at http://www.dawn.com/2004/03/10/nat3.htm

——, "Resignation not the Only Option, Says Fazl", at http://www.dawn.com/2006/11/28/top7.htm.

——, "Shujaat Rady for Talks with MMA Leaders", at http://www.dawn.com/2006/11/20/top3.htm.

——, "Treasury Withdraws Resolution in Favour of Musharraf Uniform in BA", at http://www.paktribune.com/news/.

——, "Writ at all Costs: Musharraf", at http://www.dawn.com/2006/08/28/top2.htm.

Tapper, Jake, "Spying Eyes and Ears", *Salon*, September 14, 2001, at http://dir.salon.com/politics/feature/2001/09/14/human_spies/index.html.

Wasim, Amir, "Nawaz, Qazi Agree to Launch Joint Anti-govt. Drive" at http://dawn.com/2005/01/26/top3.htm.

Yasin, Asim, "PPP has Reservations About ARD-MMA Alliance" at http:/

/www.jang.com.pk/thenews/feb2005-daily/18-02-2005/metro/i2.htm.

Yusufzai, Rahimullah, "Analysis: Pakistan's Army In the Tribal Areas", at http://www.news.bbc.co.uk/1/low/world/south_asia/3020552.html.

"3 States on US Hit-list After Iraq says Qazi", on www.dailymailnews.com/sep2002/25/main/?news=7.

"Back to Friday as Holiday", Nuggets from the Urdu Press, March 3, 2003, at http://www.thefridaytimes.com/nuggets.htm.

"Bugti Rejects Balochistan Committee's Recommendations, Aziz Assures Implementation of Balochistan Committee's Recommendations", March 22, 2005 at http://www.paktribune.com/news/index.php?id=98757

"Constitutional Status" at http://www.geocities.com/fataonline/constitutional.htm

"Enforcement of Shari'ah Act 1991", Gazette of Pakistan, Extraordinary, Part I, June 18, 1991, at http://www.pakistani.org/pakistan/legislation/1991/actXof1991.html.

"Fact Sheet: Changes to National Security Entry/Exit Registration System", Department of Homeland Security, December 1, 2003 at http://www.dhs.gov/dhspublic/display?content=3020.

"Government to Ensure Implementation of Recommendations of Parliamentary Committee on Balochistan: President, President" Press Release at http://presidentofpakistan.gov.pk/PRPressRelease

"If Iraq is Attacked, Can We be Far Behind, Ask Pakistanis" on www.navakal.com/news/regional/200212236009.asp.

"JI to Give Women Military Training", on http://www.mma.org.pk/news/2002/10/JI.

"Madrassa Registration to be discussed at NSC" at http://www.dailytimes.com.pk/default.asp?page=story_24-2-2005_pg1_7

"MMA Denies Deal, Rules Out Acceptance of Ministerial Berths" at http://paktribune.com/news/index.php?id=49975

"MMA Rejects Wana Operations" at http://www.dailytimes.com.pk/default.asp?page=story_11-1-2004-pg7_37

"MMA Supported 17th Amendment to Save System: Hafiz", at http://www.paktribune.com/news/index.php?id=83223

"MMA to Send Youth to Iraq to Fight Against US", on http://www.thenation.co.uk/kash.html.

"MMA Vows to Carry out Land Reforms", http://www.mma.org.pk/news/2002/10/mma.ows.carry.out.land.reforms.html.

"MMA Women MNAs Oppose Change to Hudood Ordinance" at http://www.dailytimes.com.pk/default.asp?page=story_10-9-2003_pg7_31

"Noorani Asks for Resotoration of 1973 Constitution", on www.mma.org.pk/news/2002/10/ Noorani.restoration.Constitution.Islamic.identity.country.html.

"Opp. MPs Slam Govt.-MMA Deal" at http://www.dailytimes.com.pk/default.asp?page=story>28-12-2003_pg7_27

"Overt Assistance from Pakistan May Bring Dire Consequences", *Jane's Intelligence Digest*, September 20, 2001, at http:///www.janes.com/security/international_security/news/jid/jid010920_1_n.html.

"Pakistan Next on US Hit list", at http://www.jamaat.org/news/pr021203.html.

"Pakistan's Militant Islamic Groups", at http://news.bbc.co.uk/1/hi/world/.

"Slogans" at http://www.mma.org.pk/campaign/2002/slogans.

"Story of Pakistan" at http://www.storyofpakistan.com/timeline12.htm.

"The Net Closes on Pakistan", at http://www.pakistan-facts.com/article.php?story=20030122091532637.

"Voices from the Whirlwind: Assessing Musharraf's Predicament", at http://www.pbs.org/frontlineworld/stories/pakistan/a.htm.

Documents and Reports

State of Democracy Report, Revival of Democracy-1st year of Democracy", November 16, 2002-November 15, 2003, Pakistan Institute for Legislative Development and Transparency (PILDAT)

State of Democracy Report, April 1, 2004-June 30, 2004, Pakistan Institute for Legislative Development and Transparency (PILDAT)

State of Democracy Report, April 1, 2004-June 30, 2004, Pakistan Institute for Legislative Development and Transparency (PILDAT)

State of Democracy Report, April 1, 2004-June 30, 2004, Pakistan Institute for Legislative Development and Transparency (PILDAT), p. 9.

State of Democracy Report, July 1, 2004-September 30, 2004, Pakistan Institute for Legislative Development and Transparency (PILDAT), p. 19.

State of Democracy Report, November 16, 2003-March 31, 2004, Pakistan Institute for Legislative Development and Transparency (PILDAT), p. 8.

State of Democracy Report, November 16, 2003-March 31, 2004, Pakistan Institute for Legislative Development and Transparency (PILDAT), p. 9. Also see Ahmed Hasan, No. 11.

State of Democracy Report, November 16, 2003-March 31, 2004, Pakistan Institute for Legislative Development and Transparency (PILDAT), p. 10.

State of Democracy Report, November 16, 2003-November 31, 2004, Pakistan Institute for Legislative Development and Transparency (PILDAT), p. 1.

Makdoom Ali Khan (ed.), *The Constitution of the Islamic Republic of Pakistan*. 1989. Pakistan Law House.

"The State of Sectarianism in Pakistan", *International Crisis Group* (ICG), Asia Report No. 95, 18 April 2005

"Pakistan: The Mullahs and the Military", *International Crisis Group* (ICG) Asia Report No. 49, 20 March 2003.

"Pakistan: Madrassas, Extremism and the Military", *International Crisis Group* (ICG), Asia Report No. 36, 29 July 2002.

K. Alan Kronstadt, Pakistan's Domestic political Developments: Issues for Congress. Congressional Research Service Report for Congress. June 19, 2003. p. CRS-6.

Poverty in Pakistan: Vulnerabilities, Social Gaps, and Rural Dynamics. World Bank Report. No. 24296. October 28, 2002.

Newspaper Articles

"Pakistan Arms Taliban by the Night", *Times of India,* November 1, 2001.

Reddy, B. Murlidhar, "Musharraf's Case Hearing" on April 22. *The Hindu*. New Delhi. April 17, 2002.

Ejaz Haider, "The Political Chessboard", *Friday Times*, February 18-24, 2005.

Hasan Mansoor, "Barelvi-Deobandi Fissure Over MMA Proposal", *The Friday Times*, September 3-9, 2004, p. 4.

K.J.M. Varma, "Musharraf can Continue as Army Chief Rules HC". *Economic Times*. 12 June 12, 2003.

M. Abul Fazal, "Feudalism". *The Nation* (Lahore). June 10 & 11, 1997.

Manoj Joshi, "Mystery Blaze Erases Pak Army's Jihadi Connection", *Times of India*, January 17, 2002.

Mazhar Abbas, "Why MQM Wants JI Banned?" *Friday Times*, July 23-29, 2004, p. 5.

Michael Meacher, *The Guardian*, July 22, 2004.

Pak Court Sets Free Jaish Chief Azhar. *Sunday Times of India*. December 15, 2002.

Strategic Foresight Group. "Window on Pakistan: Rise of Hardliners". *Times of India,* New Delhi. October 21, 2002.

Index